Advanced Introduction to Fin

Advanced Introduction to

Financial Inclusion

ROBERT LENSINK

Professor of Finance and Financial Markets, Faculty of Economics and Business, University of Groningen, Groningen, the Netherlands

CALUMN HAMILTON

Faculty of Economics and Business, University of Groningen, Groningen, the Netherlands

CHARLES ADJASI

Professor of Development Finance and Economics, University of Stellenbosch Business School, South Africa

Elgar Advanced Introductions

 **Edward Elgar**
PUBLISHING

Cheltenham, UK • Northampton, MA, USA

Published by
Edward Elgar Publishing Limited
The Lypiatts
15 Lansdown Road
Cheltenham
Glos GL50 2JA
UK

Edward Elgar Publishing, Inc.
William Pratt House
9 Dewey Court
Northampton
Massachusetts 01060
USA

A catalogue record for this book
is available from the British Library

Library of Congress Control Number: 2022937604

ISBN 978 1 83910 720 7 (cased)
ISBN 978 1 83910 721 4 (eBook)
ISBN 978 1 83910 722 1 (paperback)

Printed and bound in Great Britain by
TJ Books Ltd, Padstow, Cornwall

Contents

Figures

Tables

Focus boxes

About the authors

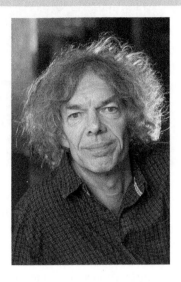

Robert Lensink is Full Professor of Finance at the Faculty of Economics and Business, University of Groningen, and a "Professor Extraordinary" at the University of Stellenbosch, South Africa. His research interest is Finance and Development, covering the broad field of financial inclusion. Robert has published widely in leading international journals like *American Economic Review, Economic Journal, Journal of Development Economics* and *World Development*.

Calumn Hamilton is a PhD candidate at the University of Groningen and an affiliate of the Groningen Growth and Development Centre. His research focuses on development economics at the macroeconomic level, including areas such as structural change, aid effectiveness, the interaction of gender and development, and financial inclusion. Calumn is also involved in the construction and maintenance of various publicly available large-scale macroeconomic databases.

Charles Adjasi is Professor of Development Finance and Economics at Stellenbosch University, an AFREXIM Bank Research Fellow and previously Visiting Professor at University of Groningen. His research focuses on financial markets, firm productivity and household welfare development in Africa. He has 50 publications, made up of 40 journal articles, four monographs and five book chapters and one coedited book.

1. Origins of financial inclusion

1.   Introduction: finance in the developing world

In March 2021, a man named Dr Abdalla Hamdok received his first Visa debit card. Dr Hamdok was at the time[1] the Prime Minister of Sudan, a country with a population of 42.8 million, and his Visa card was the first ever issued by a Sudanese bank. Not only was this Sudan's first Visa card, it was the first ever Sudanese bank card that could be used in ATMs or at PIN-point terminals outside of the country. Before the lifting of US sanctions in 2017, ATMs and retailers in Sudan could not accept any form of international bank card, and foreign visitors to the country had no option but to arrive with large stacks of cash hidden in their suitcases. To this day, outside of Khartoum, one can travel hundreds of kilometers in Sudan without ever encountering a bank branch or ATM.

Whilst Sudan is an extreme case, and Sudanese isolation from the Global Financial System was due in large part to US sanctions, this example serves to illustrate how different financial conditions can be in different parts of the world. In 2019, 185.5 billion Visa transactions were made worldwide, but zero in Sudan. Access to international financial systems may be of limited relevance to many citizens in developing countries, but international disparities extend to all aspects of the financial system, with even access to a simple deposit account at a domestic bank out of reach

---

[1]   Two weeks before submission of the final manuscript, Dr Hamdok was overthrown as Sudanese president by a military coup. Dr Hamdok was restored in power a month after the coup, but resigned in January 2022 – this serves as a stark illustration of how rapidly and unexpectedly things can change in the field of development economics!

1

for large swathes of the developing world. Such people are largely frozen out of the financial sector domestically as well as internationally. But let us back up a little bit; what is the financial sector, and why is it important?

Amoah et al. (2020) define the financial sector as "the set of institutions, markets, instruments, and the regulatory setup under which financial transactions are carried out within the financial system" (p. 20). From this definition it can be seen that the financial sector is multifaceted, and elements of it may not be obviously or immediately tangible. Banks and financial intermediation businesses are part of it, but so are the rules and conventions in which these banks and businesses operate. However, to understand the importance of the financial sector at the individual level, it is useful to visualize the lives of those with no access to it. Without access to the financial sector, all wealth must be stored as cash or physical assets, which are vulnerable to damage and theft. Savings earn no interest, and are gradually eroded by inflation. Formal credit is unavailable, so emergencies must be met with appeals to friends or family, or possibly not met at all. Productive investments beyond one's own limited earnings are a pipe-dream. Insurance is unavailable, so a single misfortune can wipe out a lifetime of accumulated assets. Buying something from a different town or village requires going physically to that town or village, or trusting your cash to an agent or transport provider. The constraints on quality of life and potential for self-advancement are obvious.

This thought exercise also serves to illustrate the importance of regulation and trust in the financial sector. In order for the financial sector to be worthwhile from the perspective of our hypothetical individual, they must be confident that their savings are *more secure* in the bank than in cash or assets. They must be confident that the debt-burden of credit will be manageable, even if they suffer some unforeseen event. They must be confident that their insurance policy will actually pay out if the contracted conditions are met, they must be confident that their financial transfer will reach their transaction interlocutor in a safe and timely manner. Therefore, nominal access to banks and financial service providers is insufficient for individuals to benefit from the financial sector without an accompanying strong institutional and regulatory framework.

The academic and policy focus on the role of the financial sector in developing countries has gone through different phases over the past decades. Tyson & Beck (2018) describe this process as "cycles of economic thought on financial sector policy" (p. 12), and provide a loosely dated typology of the different phases. They describe the 1960s and '70s as a period of *financial repression*, where developing country governments heavily intervened in financial markets with regulation and state-owned financial institutions. The 1980s, by contrast, was a period of *financial liberalization*, driven by the famous Washington Consensus,[2] whereby, in reaction to the perceived failings of the financial repression period, government intervention in financial markets in developing countries was radically stripped away in the hope that a free-as-possible market would yield a resilient and competitive financial sector. Finally, the 1990s and 2000s became something of a hybrid of the two prior regimes, where both were considered counter-productive at their most extreme, and therefore a search began to combine nuanced and limited government interventions aimed at developing and shoring up market institutions without stifling markets through interference and over-protectionism.

Whilst the Tyson & Beck (2018) chronological typography does not run into the 2010s, this most recent decade has featured a new set of developments, which adds further nuance to the descriptive analysis of normative developing country financial sector policy. Technological progress, particularly in the realm of digital and mobile communications, has broadened the set of financial sector players, and introduced a new range of platforms and tools for accessing existing and new financial products and services. Whilst the future trajectory of even newer financial technologies such as blockchain and cryptocurrencies remains unclear, the anonymity and inherent extraterritoriality of these financial innovations has the potential to dramatically reduce the ability of domestic governments and international policymakers to control the financial sector. Additionally, globalization patterns and global power structures have shifted, with China becoming a highly significant influencer of global development policy, and capital flows breaking the traditional North–South one-way street and increasingly taking place between countries in the Global South (Iacovone et al. 2013). These rapid changes present both opportunities

---

[2]   The 'Washington Consensus' was a term coined by Williamson (1990) to describe a package of 'lowest common denominator' polices prescribed by economists in the US for developing countries in Latin America. The package of policies shared a 'market liberalization' theme, and the term later became synonymous with western-advised/imposed market liberalization, often as a condition of development support, across the developing world (Williamson 2004).

and challenges for improving the positive role of finance in the developing world.

Alongside advances in global technology and shifts in global centers of power and influence, the most recent decade or two have seen changes in how academics and policymakers think about economic development. Gone is the focus purely on growth as measured by GDP per capita, replaced with a broader aim of *inclusive growth*, whereby aspects of equality, inclusivity, and standard of living are considered alongside pure GDP growth. This evolution mirrors the shift in financial sector focus from *financial development* to *financial inclusion*, as will be carefully detailed and explained in the remainder of this chapter. The chapter will proceed as follows. Section 2 introduces the concept of financial development, providing some background and history, as well as discussion over measurement and conceptual limitations. Section 3 introduces financial inclusion, providing motivation for the shift in emphasis to the financial inclusion concept, discussion over measurement issues, some key terminology, and a focused discussion on financial inclusion in Sub-Saharan Africa as compared with the rest of the developing world. Both sections 2 and 3 also provide some data and comparative empirical discussion of key financial development and inclusion indicators. Section 4 concludes with a brief summary and an overview of the key research strands that currently represent the frontier of financial inclusion research.

2.   Financial development

Financial development is a macro-concept and is considered almost exclusively in terms of broad national or regional aggregates. As with other sectoral analysis of the structure of economies, financial development is concerned primarily with the *size* or *depth* of the financial services sector as a share of the total economy (Beck et al. 1999). Standard measures of financial development include the total value added of the financial services sector as a share of GDP, private credit over GDP, or the total volume of liquid liabilities in the banking system or credit to private entities, also as shares of GDP (Allen at al. 2014; Beck et al. 1999). Thus, countries with a *larger* share of financial services or financial products in their national economies would be considered *more* financially developed, just as countries with larger shares of manufacturing would be considered more industrialized. Stock market indicators are also sometimes used, such as total market capitalization as a share of GDP or volume of trade on the stock exchange, although such measures are usually favored only when the focus is on the level of development of *institutional* finance (Amoah et al. 2020). Financial development can therefore be broadly measured by *the level of the size, depth, volume, and scope of the financial sector* or *financial services as a share of the overall national economy,* and defined as the *level of development of the financial sector within the national economy.*

In addition to the *size* or *volume* of the financial sector, researchers also sometimes consider the financial *efficiency* or financial *stability* of developing economies. Financial efficiency refers to the level of (lack of) economic distortions in financial markets, such as information problems or distortionary taxes and transaction costs. Financial stability refers to the resilience of financial sectors to economic shocks or economic crises (Beck et al. 1999). The former can to some extent be captured empirically by the level of market clearance, the latter by the volatility (standard deviation) of the aforementioned financial development indicators.[3] These factors are sometimes combined with measures of the overall size of the financial sector in order to provide a more nuanced view of the level of financial development.

This focus on financial development led first to attempts to rank countries in terms of the size of their financial sectors, then to comparison between countries and regions, and finally to evaluation of the potential determinants or constraints governing the growth of financial services sectors in developing countries (for some key papers, refer to Beck & Levine 2002, 2004; Demirgüç-Kunt & Levine 2001; King & Levine 1999).

---

[3]   Measurement and classification of financial stability is an extensively explored topic, especially but not exclusively in developed country contexts. Additional/alternative measures include shares of non-performing loans or the 'z-score' at the bank level, which measures the number of standard deviations a return realization has to fall in order to deplete equity. A higher z-score therefore implies a lower probability of insolvency. The formula for the z-score is $z=(k+\mu)/\sigma$, where k = equity capital as percentage of assets, μ is return as percentage of assets, and σ is standard deviation of return on assets as a proxy for return volatility. These measures can show us how resilient banks are to shocks and therefore how much stability is in the financial system.

As financial development is considered in terms of national aggregates, constructing such comparative data was and remains a fairly simple task – it can to a large extent be done using data directly from National Statistical Institutes (NSI) or standard secondary data sources such as the World Bank Development Indicators. Table 1.1 presents the average levels of financial development amongst lower and lower–middle income countries in different world regions according to two different measures, for every three years since 1999.[4]

Table 1.1 allows a comparison of level of financial development both between developing regions and within regions over time. It should be noted that decreases in the financial development indicators over time do not necessarily imply that the total volumes of liquid liabilities or private credit decreased, it is merely that they grew more slowly than the overall economy.

The first interesting feature of Table 1.1 is that, despite some intertemporal volatility, all six developing regions improved in terms of their level of development across the entire period of the sample. All the shares in the 2017 column are higher than the shares in the 1999 column. However, the magnitude of the improvements varies. The second interesting feature is that, by 2017, the level of financial development is quite sizeable in most regions; the share of liquid liabilities is above 50% of the economy in all but Europe & Central Asia (ECA) and Sub-Saharan Africa (SSA), and the share of private credit is above 40% in all but these two regions. This observation gives rise to the third interesting feature, which is that there is *considerable heterogeneity* between developing regions in terms of financial development performance. Note that, as the sample is restricted only to lower and lower–middle income countries, this finding is not driven by disparate numbers of rich countries in different regions of the world.

---

[4]   This temporal pattern is chosen such that the later benchmark years correspond with those of the Global Findex Survey, so as to allow easy comparison with the later presented financial inclusion indicators. Note that, in the relevant years, the numbers differ somewhat from those presented in Allen et al. (2014). These differences presumably stem from the fact that they exclude offshore financial centres, whilst we do not, and because our more recent data may include substantial historical GDP revisions for many countries (Jerven et al. 2015). However, the qualitative results in terms of ranking and gaps are the same.

Table 1.1   Evolution of aggregate financial development indicators by developing region since 1999

Liquid liabilities as share of GDP

	1999	2002	2005	2008	2011	2014	2017
East Asia & Pacific	46.1%	45.5%	41.4%	43.3%	41.6%	51.0%	57.9%
Europe & Central Asia	13.0%	21.4%	32.4%	36.7%	32.1%	38.0%	30.0%
Latin America & Caribbean	43.7%	44.0%	41.0%	44.6%	43.4%	47.8%	52.4%
Middle East and North Africa	62.3%	70.6%	73.8%	78.9%	70.7%	74.6%	86.3%
South Asia	42.3%	52.7%	56.3%	64.1%	67.1%	68.4%	68.4%
Sub-Saharan Africa	15.9%	17.2%	22.6%	22.5%	23.1%	25.1%	26.4%

Private credit from retail banks as share of GDP

	1999	2002	2005	2008	2011	2014	2017
East Asia & Pacific	30.4%	22.1%	24.9%	28.0%	31.6%	39.3%	45.8%
Europe & Central Asia	6.9%	12.8%	23.0%	51.9%	48.9%	49.8%	32.8%
Latin America & Caribbean	40.0%	35.2%	34.4%	36.5%	33.9%	39.5%	46.3%
Middle East and North Africa	39.2%	41.8%	40.5%	46.0%	40.2%	39.0%	43.0%
South Asia	21.8%	27.1%	33.1%	40.7%	43.3%	44.6%	44.0%
Sub-Saharan Africa	8.7%	8.5%	10.8%	14.7%	15.2%	15.0%	16.7%

Notes: The table shows the aggregate percentages of liquid liabilities as a share of GDP and the aggregate percentages of private credit from deposit money banks (retail banks) as a share of GDP, every three years since 1999, for each of the developing regions of the world according to the World Bank regional classifications. Only lower and lower–middle income countries are included. Data come from the World Bank Financial Structure Database and the World Bank Development Indicators. Aggregation was performed by reconstructing the total volumes of liquid liabilities and private credit, summing across regions, and dividing by the total regional GDP in current US dollars.

ECA and SSA are clear laggards in terms of financial development, at least as captured by these standard indicators. However, the low results of 30% and 32.8% for ECA in terms of liquid liabilities and private credit in 2017 seems anomalous, with the figures for 2014 being 38% and 49.8%. The former is still behind the other developing regions excluding SSA, but less markedly so, and the latter is actually greater than all other developing regions. Furthermore, ECA started from an even lower base than SSA as the region with the lowest level of financial development in 1999. Therefore, the growth over the sample period is not unsubstantial for ECA. For SSA the story is different. Whilst the level of financial development in SSA almost doubled in terms of liquid liabilities as share of GDP, and actually doubled in terms of private credit, these shares remain substantially lower than all other developing regions in all but the first year of the sample. Private credit in particular remains a very small fraction of GDP in SSA.

This negative disparity between Sub-Saharan Africa and the rest of the developing world gave rise to the concept of the *financial development gap* (Allen et al. 2014). This gap is actually more persistent even than the data in Table 1.1; it holds even after controlling for country-specific features, implying that SSA countries are and have remained behind *comparable countries*[5] in other developing regions in terms of financial development. Furthermore, as can be seen from Table 1.1, SSA has closed the gap with the other developing regions much more modestly than ECA. The SSA financial development gap is therefore of great concern to both researchers and policymakers. As will be shown later, it is also clearly visible in terms of financial inclusion. It is for this reason that so much of the empirical research into financial development and financial inclusion comes with a specific focus on Sub-Saharan Africa; this focus will also be reflected to an extent in this book. Despite this, the gap between SSA and ECA is less pronounced in the final year of the sample, 2017, especially in terms of liquid liabilities. However, this would appear to be more on account of bad performance in ECA rather than good performance in SSA. Let us hope that this blip is temporary and that future editions of this book will not be talking also about the European and Central Asian financial development gap!

---

[5]   For example, when holding constant features such as overall income level, population, natural resources etc.

The importance or relevance of financial development in overall economic development and growth has long been subject to debate. The issue can be thought of as a 'chicken-and-egg' style debate over the direction of causality; does financial development predicate growth or does growth predicate financial development? Supply-side arguments suggest that developed financial sectors are necessary for providing sources of capital, credit, and liquidity without which investment and growth cannot take place to full potential; therefore, increasing the level of financial development is a necessary condition for economic growth maximization (for a simple model linking financial development with economic growth, see Pagano (1993)). Demand-side arguments, by contrast, suggest that, as growth takes place, there is an increased demand for financial services, and as a result the financial sector develops organically so as to meet this demand (Robinson 1952).[6] There does, of course, exist a middle ground between these two positions – the bidirectional causality argument (Patrick 1966) proposes feedback loops whereby both the supply- and demand-side mechanisms are in play and financial and economic development stimulate each other in a kind of virtuous circle. This would suggest that maybe external stimulation of financial development is necessary only up to a certain threshold, after which the organic forces of supply and demand would take over. The general consensus seems to be that improving financial development can have economically meaningful impacts on growth, and that maintaining a well-functioning financial system is necessary from a growth-maximization perspective (Greenwood & Jovanovic 1990; Honohan 2004). There are, however, recent studies that cast doubt on the growth-enhancing effect of credit, and argue that the positive relationship between financial development and economic growth began to decline since the 1990s (Rousseau & Wachtel 2011). One proposed explanation for this is that, once the financial system becomes too large as compared with the domestic economy, or too complex, it becomes too vulnerable to large-scale crises, which mitigate any benefits the expansion in financial development may have (see e.g., Beck 2014). Such studies therefore demonstrate that the *nature* of increased financial development matters, and not necessarily the sheer volume.

---

[6]   A third line of argument proposes that both financial development and economic growth occur independently and that there is no causal link between the two; Lucas (1988) constructs a neoclassical model that yields such a result and argues that "importance of finance in the attainment of economic growth is badly over-stressed in popular and professional discourse."

Whilst discussion and analysis of financial development is appealing as a result of the ease of measurement, broad consensus over appropriate indicators, and the resulting consistency of comparison between countries and within countries over time, it does have severe limitations as a meaningful economic concept within the context of developing countries. By focusing exclusively on broad national aggregates, the level of financial development tells us very little about how concentrated or widespread access to financial services and financial products actually are. Whilst it may capture the *depth* of the financial system, it tells us nothing about its *breadth* (Hannig & Jansen 2010). In the context of developed economies, where it can be broadly assumed that almost all people have access to financial services at least at the commercial banking level, this distinction may be arbitrary, but in the context of developing countries this is very much not the case. Whether the vast majority of credit and/ or financial assets are held by a small number of wealthy individuals or private firms, or whether it is more spread out and accessible across the wider population, is of crucial importance to the role of finance in development. However, measures of financial development alone do not allow us to make this kind of distinction. It is for this reason that, since the early 2000s, the emphasis on exploring the role of finance in developing countries has shifted from the macro-level concept of financial development to the more micro concept of *financial inclusion*.

3.   Financial inclusion

3.1   What is financial inclusion?

To illustrate the shortcomings of the *financial development* concept, and the resulting necessity of a shift in focus towards *financial inclusion*, it is useful to consider the World Bank Universal Financial Access by 2020 goal.

> The UFA goal is that by 2020, adults, who currently aren't part of the formal financial system, are able to have access to a transaction account to store money, send and receive payments as the basic building block to manage their financial lives .... The World Bank Group has committed to enabling 1 billion people to gain access to a transaction account through targeted interventions. (World Bank 2018)

The motivation for this goal is that financial access has been identified as an enabler for seven of the 17 Sustainable Development Goals. However, it will be immediately apparent that none of the aforementioned financial development measures or concepts tells us anything meaningful regarding progress towards this goal. Without exploring the *breadth* of the financial system, we know little about how many people have access to, or make use of, financial services, regardless of their size or volume as a share of the economy. And without knowing how many people are able to actually access or use the financial system, we have no idea how *inclusive* it is.

Precise definitions of *financial inclusion* differ, but thinking of the financial sector in terms of individuals and access rather than countries and dollars is the common theme. The reason for the variation in definitions is that, at the individual level, financial inclusion can incorporate a variety of different concepts and concerns. Chapter 2 will lay out some of these in more detail. A good working definition that corresponds broadly with the UFA2020 goal is, "[financial inclusion involves] broadening access, availability, and enhancing the usage of formal financial services by all segments of the population" (Sarma 2008, p. 3). However, countries often adopt their own definitions of financial inclusion so as to better incorporate the specific context and financial needs of their population. Some definitions prefer to explicitly incorporate equality of access to financial services along lines such as ethnicity and gender (Leyshon and Thrift 1995).

3.2   Evolving measurement issues

At this point, one might ask why the shift in focus from financial development to financial inclusion occurred only relatively recently, given the importance of financial inclusion. A recently enhanced understanding of the fundamental role of inclusivity and equality in economic development is certainly part of the explanation. However, as with many topics in empirical economic development, the concepts and analysis can only progress as far as there are adequate data available. One of the advantages of analyzing financial development was the relative ease with which data could be constructed and compared; this has not always been the case with analysis of financial inclusion. It will not surprise the reader that, within developing country contexts, accurate and useable data on *individuals* are much more difficult to find and construct than data on the country as a whole.

In order to overcome this hurdle, the first generation of financial inclusion research, as with financial development research, concerned itself primarily with broad national aggregates. These retain the 'macro-style' country-level approach and can be broadly described as 'supply-side' measures because they relate to breadth of the supply of financial products and services in countries and regions. Such data can often be collected from NSI household survey publications or from the more specific Financial Access Survey of the IMF (IMF 2020). Examples of supply-side measures of financial inclusion would include variables such as bank branches per capita or per square kilometer, total number of bank accounts per capita, or average (opportunity) costs of accessing or utilizing financial services. It can immediately be seen how such measures can be better utilized for evaluating the breadth of financial access than those of financial development. By examining such variables, we can gain some impression of the extent to which access to financial services is likely concentrated amongst the many or the few.

Despite the improvements represented by this first generation of measures, many limitations still remained. Broad country aggregates such as bank accounts per capita or per square kilometer tell us little about the spatial or social dispersion of access to financial services. A country with a large number of bank branches concentrated in major cities, but almost none in rural areas, would appear to offer a high level of financial sector access at the country level, but this access could not be considered comprehensive or inclusive. Similarly, if we merely know the total bank accounts per capita, we will not be aware of situations where women, ethnic minorities, or residents of certain regions or terrains are left behind in terms of their access to the financial system. Additionally, by looking purely at the *volume* of bank accounts, we gain no information as to how intensively they are actually being used. Some may not even be active at all. This touches on the difference between *access* and *use*, which will be further elaborated in the next chapter. Finally, bank accounts and individuals by no means correspond; countries where some individuals and businesses hold multiple bank accounts and others hold none may appear to offer much wider financial access than they actually do in reality. It is clear that, for an individual-level concept such as financial inclusion, individual-level 'micro-style' data become necessary, and this need predicated the second generation of financial inclusion indicators, which can be thought of as 'demand-side' measures.

Whereas supply-side measures of financial inclusion relate to the breadth of the supply of financial services within a country, demand-side measures relate to the *level of demand* for such services by *individuals* within countries. So individuals, or shares of total individuals, become the units of measurement. Examples include the *share of total individuals* in a country who hold a bank account, utilize credit, used their bank account within, say, the last three months, or utilized some other financial product or service. When stratified by gender, age, ethnicity, or location, such measures can also be compared *within* countries *between* social groups.

It will be immediately apparent that such measures can be used to create a far more complete picture of the true degree of inclusivity of the financial sector within countries and regions. If such measures are so useful for evaluating financial inclusion, why then were they not used from the beginning? There are two reasons for this. The first is that gains in conceptual precision are to some extent mitigated by losses in terms of comparability. The issue here is that such demand-side financial inclusion measures are fundamentally multi-dimensional. If country A performs better in terms of share of individuals with an active bank account, but country B performs better in terms of share of individuals who access loans and credit, how do we adjudicate which of the two countries is 'more' financially inclusive? Whilst different financial development measures will broadly correlate, this may not be the case for demand-side financial inclusion measures. Attempts have been made to combine such indicators into unidimensional indices (Sarma 2008), but such indices will by nature involve subjective decision-making by the researchers who construct them. As the literature evolves, broader consensus over the most relevant indicators or preferable indices may emerge, but for now the use of such indicators remains problematic for 'clear and easy' international comparison.

The second impediment to earlier adoption of demand-side measures of financial inclusion was, and to some extent remains, data availability. Individual-level indicators require individual-level data, and such data have long been elusive in the developing country context. To this end, the release of the first version of the World Bank Global Findex Database (GFD) in 2011 can be thought of as a watershed moment. The GFD is a large-scale multi-country survey designed with the specific purpose of eliciting "how adults save, borrow, make payments, and manage risk" (Demirgüç-Kunt et al. 2017, p. xv). The release of these data for 140 different countries meant that demand-side financial inclusion indicators of the type discussed above were available in a consistent, cross-country form for the first time. The second and third rounds of the GFD survey were conducted in 2014 and 2017, with the scheduled 2020 round delayed on account of the Covid-19 pandemic. With multiple releases comes the opportunity to evaluate changes in financial inclusion within countries and regions over time. However, within each country, the individuals comprising each sample survey are not the same for each release, rendering it impossible to use panel data techniques at the individual level to uncover dynamic changes over time. Similarly, at present the total time period covered by the surveys remains relatively short, limiting the potential to analyze long-term changes and trends. Despite this, the GFD remains the 'gold-standard' data source for analysis of financial inclusion, and the range of research avenues that have become unblocked as a result of these data cannot be overstated.

3.3   Who delivers financial inclusion?

So who are the major players in developing country financial markets? *Commercial banks* come to mind first when conceptualizing providers of financial products and services. In some developing countries, commercial banks are fully or partially nationalized; in others they operate purely as private enterprises. Hybrid systems of nationalized and private banks are especially common in the countries of South Asia; this gives these governments strong influence over commercial banking activities (Pandey et al. 2020). Whilst commercial banks are a minority of total deposit-taking institutions (DTI) in most developing regions, a much larger share of total DTI assets is concentrated in the hands of the largest banks (Hawkins and Mihaljek 2001). Therefore, the largest banks tend to be the biggest players in developing country financial markets when considered by volumes of assets and liabilities. Despite this, commercial banks and their more traditional business model is generally not optimal for the purpose of delivering financial inclusion.[7] Mas (2011) describes the retail role of banks from the perspective of most people in developing countries as the conversion of the physical to the electronic, and

---

[7]   There are some exceptions to this, such as the example of Equity Bank discussed in Focus Box 1.1. However, these exceptions usually involve deliberate or accidental deviation from standard commercial retail banking practices and business models.

vice-versa. That is, physical cash is deposited and becomes numbers on an electronic banking ledger, or withdrawn with the result that those electronic numbers go down. Credit creates an electronic asset in the banks' digital ledger whilst handing out physical cash to the borrower. This is different from retail banking in developed countries where most transfers go from electronic to electronic: salaries are deposited electronically into bank accounts, spent electronically at pin-point terminals, or transferred electronically to pay bills and other obligations. Physical transfers require physical locations, and the physical locations of the standard commercial banking model are branches and ATMs. These come with high fixed costs, staffing, and infrastructure requirements. Bank branches require specialist locations with sophisticated security and educated staff, ATMs require constant oversight and maintenance, and both are dependent on electricity, digital connectivity, and physical road access by armored, cash-carrying vehicles. For a branch or ATM to be profitable, therefore, it needs to generate such large returns as to overcome all of these fixed and variable costs, and in some cases the infrastructure requirements are beyond the influence of banks even if they otherwise want to open a branch or ATM. This explains the high concentration of commercial bank branches and ATMs in major cities, and their relative paucity in rural, impoverished, or unstable areas.

Aware of these limitations and of the inability to serve potentially profitable, unbanked customers in lower-density or lower-infrastructure areas, some banks have changed the nature of their physical locations along with their product offerings. *Microfinance banks* can be offshoots of existing commercial banks or entirely new entities. Additionally, microfinance banks, or microfinance institutions (MFIs), are frequently conduits for international development policy. Banco Azteca in Mexico, as studied by Bruhn & Love (2014) in a paper discussed extensively in Chapter 3, is an example of a commercial bank that adopted a largely MFI-style business model. For the most part, however, MFIs are separate institutions from commercial banks. The origins of microfinance can be traced back to 19th-century European farmers' credit co-operatives (Suesse & Wolf 2020). However, the emergence of microfinance as a primary weapon in the fight against global poverty is relatively recent – the seeds of the 'microfinance revolution' could be said to have been sown in 1976 when Muhammad Yunus made his first loan of $27 to a group of stool makers in Bangladesh, and grown into tall trees by 2006 when Yunus won the Nobel Peace Prize (Sengupta & Aubuchon 2008). Indeed, we may well have observed a subsequent counter-revolution when numerous scholars and policymakers began to question the ethics and efficacy of microfinance as a tool for poverty reduction (Ellerman 2007; Meyer 2007; Hudon & Sandberg 2013). Yet, MFIs remain the most prominent providers of financial products and services in developing countries with an *explicit financial inclusion focus*, and most policy efforts at expanding access to and use of the financial system have been channeled through MFIs.

To give a full overview of the history, nature, and role of microfinance and MFIs is beyond the scope of this book. The interested reader can consult Robinson (2001), both as a detailed description of what microfinance is, and as a normative, theory-backed manifesto for the importance of microfinance as a global development tool. Sengupta & Aubuchon (2008) provides a somewhat more hedged, but still optimistic, overview of the 'microfinance revolution' in the years after Yunus's Nobel Prize, whilst Dichter & Harper (2007) collates microfinance critiques. Hudon et al. (2019) brings the story of development microfinance up to date and provides a new research agenda for the interplay of microfinance and financial inclusion; this includes Garcia & Lensink (2019), which charts the evolution from microfinance to 'microfinance plus' and details the extension of the sets of products and services offered by MFIs. For recent overviews, we also refer to Armendáriz & Morduch (2010), Hermes & Lensink (2007, 2020), and Lensink & Bulte (2019). These references underly the overview in the next paragraph.

In brief, MFIs provide small-scale basic financial services such as credit and savings to low-income populations. The small size of the sums involved, and relative simplicity of the range of services, reduces the risks and the costs to MFIs – credit risk is spread over a large amount of small-scale borrowers such that individual defaults are less damaging, smaller sums require less physical security, and simple products do not require such highly educated MFI staff or sophisticated digital networks. Lower risks allow for acceptance of a wider range of borrowers or depositors without collateral – people who would not be accepted as customers of most commercial banks. Lower costs allow for MFI outlets to be set up in more low-density and isolated locations, because large branches can be replaced with smaller 'pop-up' style counters and simple transactions can be recorded without sophisticated digital infrastructure. Simpler products can be easily explained to potential customers with lower levels of formal education who may be initially skeptical of the financial sector.

All of these are reasons why MFIs are able to reach a broader set of the population than commercial banks, and are therefore seen as tools for boosting levels of financial inclusion. Discussion of the impacts and efficacy of the increases in financial inclusion facilitated by MFIs is held over until Chapter 3.

Alongside commercial banks and MFIs, the other major entities involved in delivering financial inclusion are governments, international organizations and NGOs, and, increasingly, technology providers. Developing country governments can boost financial inclusion both as a result of explicit financial inclusion policy goals, and as a byproduct of other policies. An example of the latter would be if government transfers such as pension payments or tax refunds required a bank account in order to receive the funds; in this case broader sections of the population would be incentivized to join the banking system even if this was not the primary policy intention. In the case of the former, governments can use their monopoly power over the issuance of banking licences to pressure commercial banks into more inclusive practices (Burgess & Pande 2005), or set up or subsidize MFIs of their own. Of course, such interventions can introduce severe distortions into the financial market and must be done with extreme care (Helms 2006). Arun & Kamath (2015) provides an extensive overview of different, and often disparate, strategies undertaken by national governments with the goal of increasing financial inclusion, whilst highlighting the importance of taking local context into account when designing FI policy.

Similarly, international organizations (IOs) and NGOs increasingly regard financial inclusion as a primary development goal in its own right, as well as a tool towards other development aims; cf. the discussion of the sustainable development goals at the beginning of section 3.1 (World Bank 2018). These IOs and NGOs may lack direct access to the levers of control over the financial sector held by national governments, but they make up for it with extensive international donor funding. IOs and NGOs frequently provide financial support for setting up new MFIs and subsidize those already in existence, and can therefore exert quite considerable influence over developing country MFI sectors (Khawari 2004; Helms 2006). A major advantage of financial inclusion interventions by international development actors from a research perspective is that they often build in rigorous impact evaluations; many of the findings discussed in Chapter 3 are a result of this practice. Of course, the same caveats regarding introducing distortions into financial markets apply for international development actors as for governments; whilst they may have a lesser capacity to introduce distortions via rules and regulations, the vast capital flows involved and implicit subsidies they represent clearly has ripple effects across the entire local financial sector. Whilst self-sustainability is a key tenet of most international microfinance interventions (Dunford 2003), the initial financial backing of these institutions, and underwriting of poor performing loans etc., can be extremely high.

Finally, in an increasingly digital world, technology and technology providers are taking an ever-larger role in the provision of broader access to financial products and services, either in conjunction with existing banks and MFIs (such as through online banking) or as separate entities. The above discussed 'physical-to-electronic' core of retail banking in developing counties (Mas 2011) may finally be weakening as mobile phone ownership and cellular internet access proliferate. 'Mobile money' services, provided mostly by telecommunications companies although sometimes in conjunction with banks, allow for increasingly complex financial transactions to be performed with nothing but a mobile phone (Hinson et al. 2019). This provides rudimentary financial sector access to large swathes of the unbanked, provided they live in an area with cellphone coverage and can afford a basic mobile phone.[8] This is still by no means everyone in the developing world, and many of the most impoverished and financially excluded remain outside of this category. Nevertheless, mobile money has had considerable success in penetrating previously unbanked population segments in some countries. Further digital technologies may yield further potential for financial inclusion in the 21st century; under the broad category of FinTech, Chapter 6 will explore the potential, and potential pitfalls, of these technologies in greater detail.

3.4   Who *should* deliver financial inclusion?

Now that we know who *are* the major players in delivering financial inclusion across the developing world, we approach the more difficult normative question of who *should* deliver financial inclusion. Where does the responsibility for bringing the financially excluded into the financial

---

[8]   Most mobile money transactions do not require a smartphone and can be done with the most basic handset provided there is cellular, not necessarily 3G, coverage.

system lie? Is it right that governments and international organizations intervene in financial sectors to financially include individuals when the existing market does not deem it profitable to do so? Where should the funds for financial inclusion (FI) interventions come from? There is by no means consensus in opinion over questions such as these, and we choose not to go into too much detail around these debates here, preferring merely to make the reader aware of these questions so that they can then consider them in the light of the forthcoming discussions of this book. Nevertheless, the principle dialectic in the normative consideration of the provision of financial inclusion is between FI as a responsibility of governments and FI as a product of the private sector.

Aggarwal & Klapper (2013) list the various obstacles to financial inclusion in developing countries and argue that they are insurmountable without government intervention; this tacitly invokes the prohibitive initial fixed costs of providing financial access to a large proportion of the citizenry, despite the fact that variable costs may be low thereafter. Chibba (2009) issues something of a call to arms to the international community to provide financial inclusion, arguing that FI is a key intermediate step in path towards achieving many of the Millennium Development Goals (MDGs), and therefore the acceptance of the MDGs as the responsibility of international organizations is tantamount to also accepting responsibility for financial inclusion. In contrast, Mohiuddin (2015), whilst accepting the social necessity of financial inclusion as an international goal, argues that it is now time for the private sector to come to the fore in the provision of FI, listing a number of successful FI innovations that came about as a result of market needs and mechanisms. Gabor & Brooks (2017) note the game-changing role of the digital revolution in the provision of financial inclusion and the fact that new technologies may render obsolete traditional international development FI tools such as microfinance banks. Finally, Ozili (2020) notes that the level of financial inclusion in a country is strongly underpinned by conditions in the private financial sector of that country such as financial sector innovation, stability, and regulation. The implication of this is that ignoring the private financial sector in the focus on boosting FI may be counter-productive if it undermines the very conditions required for sustainable financial inclusion. This paper also notes the *community echelon theory* of financial inclusion, which highlights the need to take local leadership structures into account when optimally dispersing financial inclusion products and programs; something that homogeneous international policymakers or even national governments may be insufficiently localized to do. Focus Box 1.1 explores in more depth the specific example of Equity Bank in Kenya, as studied in an important paper by Allen at al. (2021), in order to demonstrate that, at least in some instances, reaching out with new services to the financially excluded and increasing private banking profits can be positively symbiotic.

To bring this brief summary of the normative debate to a close, one is essentially caught between the difference in private and social returns to boosting financial inclusion on the one hand, and the potentially superior ability of the market to innovate and develop new forms of financial products and services on the other. Where there is a difference between private and social returns, there is an externality, and where there is an externality, there is a strong case for government intervention. However, as discussions in the focus boxes and following chapters will make clear, identifying where there is latent demand for financial services, and which kinds of services people actually want, is a difficult task and prone to errors and missteps. Some may argue that market mechanisms combined with technological innovations have a better long-run chance of identifying and filling these gaps, and the aforementioned FI externality can be better internalized by supporting these private sector forces rather than imposing competing publicly funded solutions.

Focus box 1.1   Is increasing financial inclusion good business or just good charity? The case of Equity Bank

At this point, some readers might be asking themselves whether expanding financial inclusion is inherently a charitable or non-profit exercise, or if doing so can actually be 'good business' from the perspective of the financial service providers. It might appear that, if certain strata of a country are currently underserved by financial services, this must be because it is not profitable to serve them without external incentives or subsidies. It is certainly the case that many attempts to boost financial inclusion require international funding or state intervention (Burgess & Pande 2005), although these may still be profitable from a societal perspective if the long-term effect is to boost economic outcomes. However, an important recent paper by Allen et al. (2021)

demonstrates that, in some circumstances, expanding financial inclusion can also be profitable and optimal from the purely private perspective of financial service providers.

Focusing on one locally owned bank in Kenya – Equity Bank – Allen et al. (2021) shows first that this bank pursued a deliberate strategy from 2006 onwards of expanding into previously unbanked and non-central locations. During this time period Equity Bank also experienced enormous growth and commercial success, with the stock price increasing by 900% in the decade since 2006 – considerably more than other banks in Kenya of all types. The paper goes on to use financial inclusion measures of the type discussed in Chapter 2 to show that the post-2006 branch expansion considerably increased financial inclusion in the regions where the new bank branches were opened. Most importantly, the paper shows that the new branches in previously unbanked areas were *more profitable* than new branches in urban areas that were already well served with banks, a result that is consistent across a variety of profit measures and robust to a battery of sophisticated econometric techniques.

How can it be that these bank branches in areas that other banks had considered not worthwhile turned out to be more profitable than new branches in well-banked areas? The authors demonstrate that the explanation is, in part, precisely *because* there were no other banks in these areas, meaning that, when Equity Bank became the first, they had a high degree of market power. It is shown that the interest rates paid on deposits were lower at these branches than elsewhere, and that the interest rates charged on loans were higher (although not exploitatively high), resulting in a higher profit margin for the bank. It was because of the lack of competition that Equity Bank could employ this less-competitive pricing of their financial products and services. The other half of the explanation comes from Equity Bank's approach to expansion, whereby there was a strong focus on harnessing local knowledge and speaking local languages within the staff of the new bank branches. As a locally owned bank, Equity Bank was able or willing to do this much more effectively than their competitors, with the result that loan delinquency rates were *lower* in the new branches in the previously unbanked areas. It is also shown that branches in areas with minority languages were *even more profitable*; further evidence of the positive effect of the local-knowledge and local-language approach.

The above findings, and explanations for these findings, paint both an optimistic and a pessimistic view of the potential profitability of expanding financial inclusion. The fact that a bank was able to carry out an expansion strategy in which rapidly increasing financial inclusion was both commercially possible, and commercially very profitable, is an extremely positive finding, and shows definitively that there is a model through which financial inclusion and profit-maximizing banking can go hand in hand. However, the scope of this model must be called into question – if the reason for the profitability effect is due to the lack of competition, there are obvious limits on the potential for other banks to also get in on the action, and the profitability effect may rapidly disappear if other banks do start to serve these areas. Furthermore, if local knowledge is a prerequisite to profitable banking in previously unbanked areas, countries with financial sectors dominated by foreign-owned banks, or without sufficient human capital to provide qualified local banking staff, will not be able to replicate the profitable Equity Bank model. A final important point of note is that the time period of this study, ending in 2009, is before mobile banking really took off in Kenya; this phenomenon may have broken the essential link between physical access to bank branches and access to banking services. Still, this excellent and comprehensive paper provides definitive evidence that there are at least some circumstances in which increasing financial inclusion can be profitable for banks in the short term as well as for individuals and society in the long term.

4. Conclusion

This chapter has laid the groundwork for a deeper exploration of financial inclusion in development policy, research, and in the developing world. It can be seen that financial inclusion has its origins in, but is distinct from, financial development, and requires a different set of tools and concepts both for descriptive analysis and for normative policy prescription.

The current state of the financial inclusion literature renders it one of the most exciting fields within empirical development economics. Despite decades of interest in the role of finance and the financial sector in development, the financial inclusion literature remains relatively nascent and it is only within the last few years that the necessary tools have become available to really take our understanding of financial inclusion forward. Two major advances were necessary for the study of financial inclusion to reach its current, exciting state. First, the importance and relevance of financial inclusion, rather than financial development, had to be established as an academic consensus, with corresponding appropriate definitions and measures of financial inclusion. Second, suitable data were necessary such that financial inclusion could be explored and compared in a consistent and meaningful way between countries and over time, and such that the tools of statistical and econometric inference could be applied to the study of financial inclusion. The Global Findex Database (GFD) provided the key to unlock this latter advance, and as more rounds of the GFD become available, the potential for analysis will further expand.

The next chapter will drill down deeper into the specific concepts and definitions necessary to fully understand and participate in academic and policy conversations around financial inclusion, before providing a first pass over the GFD data in order to present the 'state of the world' as it currently is in terms of financial inclusion, as well as how it has evolved in recent years. This chapter will then present and discuss the main determinants of financial inclusion. Subsequent chapters will explore the impacts of financial inclusion via an overview of the theoretical and empirical literature thus far; the crucial interplay between financial inclusion, gender, and women empowerment; and the future of financial inclusion, particularly in relation to technology and FinTech.

2. Financial inclusion: concepts, empirics, and determinants

1. Introduction

In 2010 in Burundi, a country with a population of 8 million, the largest bank had a total of 33 branches and two ATMs. All banks combined had a total of just over 100 points of presence – one per 80,000 people. Less than one tenth of the population participated in the formal banking system, and were almost all at the top of the income distribution (Mas 2011). But commercial banks are not the only providers of financial products and services. Burundi has hosted some form of microfinance institutions (MFIs) since 1964, but in the period 2004–2009 the value of microfinance loans issued quadrupled, whilst the number of MFI members increased by almost 60%, and the number of MFI employees doubled (Nkurunziza et al. 2012). By 2013, the commercial bank branches per capita had increased by 50%, overtaking neighboring Tanzania and nearby Uganda, before flatlining until 2016 – the last year of available data (IMF 2020). In 2010, mobile money did not exist in Burundi, but in 2012 Burundi's largest bank partnered with Burundi's largest telecommunications provider to launch MobiCash, and already by 2014, 6 percent of Burundians used a mobile phone to receive international remittances.[1] Were these the same people who were already amongst the small minority of formal banking users, were they already MFI members, or did the advent of mobile money bring a new set of individuals into the financial system?

---

[1]   According to 2014 Global Findex Data.

How can we best tell the complicated story of financial inclusion in Burundi? It is clear that, in order to do so, we are going to need a toolbox of concepts and measures, as well as some theoretical and empirical understanding of drivers and determinants. Clearly focusing on supply-side measures such as bank branches per capital or volume of MFI loans does not tell the whole story, so instead we need to look at *individuals* and at the demand side. And before we start to count or apportion individuals, we need to understand them. Who are the people who are not participating in the financial system, and why? Is their exclusion voluntary or involuntary, idiosyncratic or systematic, a product of discrimination or of market forces? Along which dimensions, if any, are they financially included, and which of these dimensions of financial inclusion are increasing more rapidly? Finally, what *determines* whether or not they are financially included, and how can these barriers to financial inclusion be overcome?

This chapter builds on the introduction to the origins of financial inclusion policy and research developed in Chapter 1 and aims to provide a richer toolbox for understanding these complex phenomena. By introducing the reader to the key concepts of financial inclusion, we not only lay out a common vocabulary but also uncover the subtle distinctions that underly theoretical and empirical research. A first pass over the financial inclusion data then serves to familiarize the reader with the current 'state of play' in the world with regards to financial inclusion, what progress has been made and has not been made in the most recent years, and where the biggest differences and disparities – 'the gaps' – lie. Finally, a dive into the determinants of financial inclusion provides some guidance as to how financial inclusion policy must be designed, why the observed gaps have materialized, and how we might go about closing them in a sustainable manner.

2.   Key concepts in financial inclusion

Before moving on to a first pass over the actual Global Findex Database (GFD) data, it is useful to first state and elaborate some key concepts within the study of financial inclusion. As demonstrated above, financial inclusion is a multi-dimensional and multi-faceted concept, and familiarity with these concepts may guide the reader in terms of what to look for in the data and which empirical questions may later become important.

The distinction between *access* to and *use* of financial services was touched upon before in Chapter 1 of this book. Access refers to the breadth of the population who *potentially could* utilize financial products and services if they want to, whereas use refers to the breadth of the population who *actually do* utilize them. *Intensity of use* refers to how regularly or up to what value the average person utilizes financial products and services. Those who do not use any financial products or services are often referred to collectively as *the unbanked*, and are considered *excluded* from the financial system. This group can be subdivided into *voluntarily excluded* and *involuntarily excluded*, whereby the former group could access financial products and services if they wanted to but choose not to, and the latter group would like to access financial products or services but cannot because they do not have access to them, are explicitly or implicitly barred from them, or find them prohibitively expensive or complicated. Broadly speaking, in terms of individuals, the difference between access and use is the voluntarily excluded.

Systematic, or *structural, involuntary exclusion* refers to the situation when specific social groups or population subgroups are involuntarily excluded from the financial system in a biased manner. This may be as a result of deliberate prejudice or discrimination against, for example, minority ethnic groups, or it may be as a result of other factors, such as when certain subgroups live predominantly in the geographic periphery. Even when deliberate discrimination is absent, a financial sector that cares less about appealing to some subgroups as compared with others may result in financial access that is systematically inadequately dispersed. Additionally, statistical discrimination may take place whereby, when there is asymmetric information regarding the quality of the borrower, or the possibility for moral hazard, average group statistics such as propensity for default are used as proxies for individual characteristics (Akerlof 1976). See Focus Box 2.1 for a further explanation of why involuntary exclusion may take place in credit markets. *Systematic voluntary exclusion* is also possible, whereby specific population subgroups systematically choose not to access financial products and services for cultural reasons; for example, some religions prohibit borrowing or lending when interest is charged. Even though such exclusion is voluntary, it can still sometimes be reduced if the financial sector offers products or services that are more tailored to the preferences of specific subgroups.

Finally, it is important to note that all of the above measures and discussion of financial inclusion refer exclusively to the *formal* financial sector. Most developing countries, however, also contain extensive *informal* financial sectors, the scale and value of which is often severely under-captured in the national accounts (Hussmanns 2005). The informal financial sector ranges from simple credit at local shops or loans from unlicensed moneylenders to fairly sophisticated savings organizations and 'games' such as *rotating credit and savings associations* (ROSCAs), whereby members pay in small amounts of money every few days in order to receive a large amount of money more infrequently when their turn comes up. The existence of these informal financial sectors can both mitigate and exacerbate problems of financial inclusion. On the positive side, by allowing the leveraging of local knowledge and informal reputational networks, they can provide a form of financial service to those excluded from the formal financial system, and sometimes even can offer cheaper credit or other services to certain individuals (Manig 1990). Additionally, there is some evidence that the informal financial sector may partially redress gender imbalances in financial inclusion, as ROSCA membership is much more common amongst women than men (Anderson & Baland 2002). On the negative side, when financial services are informal and unmonitored, the potential for exploitation and predatory lending is far greater, as are outright forms of discrimination and prejudice. In summary, the first best optimum would probably be a well-functioning formal financial sector that renders the need for an informal sector redundant, but in the absence of this, certain types of co-operative informal finance may represent second-best optima when compared with situations where there are no financial services at all.

Focus box 2.1   **Information asymmetry and involuntary exclusion from the credit market**

The seminal paper by Stiglitz and Weiss (1981) provides an analytical framework that clearly show why financial markets differ from normal markets of goods and services. They hypothesize that informational problems may induce banks to ration credit. The main reasons are that increases in the interest rate not only lead to a decrease in demand for credit but may needlessly attract more risky borrowers (adverse selection) and induce existing borrowers to invest in riskier projects (moral hazard), both of which may lead to increases in the overall rate of defaults. The implication then may be that an increase in the interest rate will not lead to a monotonic increase in bank returns; it may even lead to a decline in bank returns when increases in the default rate dominate, as is depicted in the left-hand panel of Figure 2.1. The non-monotonic bank return curve will lead to a supply curve that is backward bending at the optimal interest rate, as is depicted in the right-hand panel of Figure 2.1. If the demand for credit is given by the demand curve in the picture below, banks will decide to ration at the optimal interest rate r^* as an increase in the interest rate above r^* will lower bank returns.

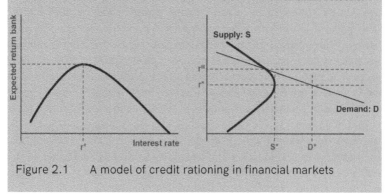

Figure 2.1   A model of credit rationing in financial markets

3.   Data and analysis

The Global Findex Database has quickly become the gold-standard source for empirical exploration and analysis of financial inclusion. This section will begin to explore these data, and data and analysis from this source will reappear throughout this book. At this stage, the most important selection criteria of variables for empirical comparison is comparability across studies; for this reason, the indicators we present correspond with those in Allen et al. (2014). They are the *proportion of individuals* with a bank account at a formal financial institution, and the *proportion of individuals* who received a loan in the 12 months prior to the survey. The repeated emphasis via italics is to reiterate the point that this is individual micro-level data scaled up to regional-level aggregates. Table 2.1 presents these results by region for the overall population, Table 2.2 presents the *differential* results between men and women. High-income countries are excluded from the sample, and the population refers only to individuals aged 15 or above.

Table 2.1   Evolution of aggregate financial inclusion indicators by developing region since 2011

Men and women

Share of 15+ individuals with a formal bank account

	2011	2014	2017
East Asia & Pacific	55%	69%	71%
Europe & Central Asia	45%	58%	65%
Latin America & Caribbean	39%	51%	54%
Middle East and North Africa	33%	N/A	43%
South Asia	32%	47%	70%
Sub-Saharan Africa	23%	34%	43%

Share of 15+ individuals who received a formal loan in the previous 12 months

	2011	2014	2017
East Asia & Pacific	9%	11%	11%
Europe & Central Asia	8%	12%	13%
Latin America & Caribbean	8%	11%	9%
Middle East and North Africa	12%	N/A	8%
South Asia	9%	6%	7%
Sub-Saharan Africa	5%	6%	7%

Notes: The table shows the aggregate share of individuals with a bank account at a formal financial institution and the aggregate share of individuals who received a formal loan in the 12 months prior to the survey, every three years since 2011, for each of the developing regions of the world according to the World Bank regional classifications. High-income countries and individuals under 15 years old are excluded. Data come from the World Bank Global Findex Database utilizing the regional aggregates as provided.

The regional structure of Table 2.1 allows us to compare the level of financial inclusion between developing regions. Whilst only three rounds of the Global Findex Survey have thus far been conducted, the fact that there are three different survey years allows for comparison of the evolution of financial inclusion between and within developing regions over time, albeit across a somewhat compact time period. Table 2.2 allows us to assess the evolution of the *gender gap* in financial inclusion both between regions and within regions over time.

Focusing first on Table 2.1, it may come as a pleasant surprise that, even within the relatively short sample period of only six years, all developing regions experienced a marked increase in the share of individuals with a bank account between 2011 and 2017. This level of growth is not, however, replicated in the share of individuals with a loan, where gains are much more modest in most regions, and there is actually a decline in the share of the population with a loan in the Middle East and North Africa (MENA) and South Asia (SA). This finding combined with the low absolute values for the shares of individuals with a loan in all regions suggests that improving access to credit is a much more stubborn task than improving access to retail banking services. Such a result is one motivating factor for unconventional policy approaches to the provision of credit in developing countries, such as Microfinance.

From Table 2.1, as in Table 1.1 for financial development, the gap between Sub-Saharan Africa (SSA) and other developing regions can be observed, although in the most recent survey year, 2017, SSA has actually drawn level with MENA in terms of share of individuals with a bank account. As this appears to be due to growth in SSA rather than decline in MENA, this is a tentatively positive finding for the reduction of the SSA financial inclusion gap. The gap is less observable in terms of share of individuals with a loan; whilst SSA remains tied in last place with SA in terms of this indicator in 2017, the gap is to an extent overshadowed by the relatively poor performance of all developing regions in terms of inclusivity of credit. A full introductory discussion of Sub-Saharan Africa and the financial inclusion gap will take place in the next section, and the concept will be revisited elsewhere in this book.

Turning now to Table 2.2, we see perhaps the most sobering finding of this initial data exploration from the gender dimension of financial inclusion. Every differential, in every region, in every survey year is negative,

Table 2.2   Evolution of gender differential between aggregate financial inclusion indicators by developing region since 1999

Gender differential (women – men)

Share of 15+ individuals with a formal bank account

	2011	2014	2017
East Asia & Pacific	-5.7%	-4.0%	-5.3%
Europe & Central Asia	-9.9%	-2.7%	-6.1%
Latin America & Caribbean	-9.3%	-5.7%	-6.5%
Middle East and North Africa	-14.6%	N/A	-17.4%
South Asia	-15.9%	-17.7%	-10.9%
Sub-Saharan Africa	-5.0%	-8.6%	-11.5%

Share of 15+ individuals who received a formal loan in the previous 12 months

	2011	2014	2017
East Asia & Pacific	-1.6%	-1.6%	-2.6%
Europe & Central Asia	-1.0%	-1.1%	-2.7%
Latin America & Caribbean	-0.9%	-2.8%	-2.1%
Middle East and North Africa	-2.1%	N/A	-2.0%
South Asia	-1.6%	-2.6%	-2.8%
Sub-Saharan Africa	-1.0%	-1.1%	-1.9%

Notes: The table shows the gender differential between the aggregate share of women and men with a bank account at a formal financial institution and the aggregate share of women and men who received a formal loan in the 12 months prior to the survey, every three years since 2011, for each of the developing regions of the world according to the World Bank regional classifications. High-income countries and individuals under 15 years old are excluded. Data come from the World Bank Global Findex Database utilizing the regional aggregates as provided; the gender differential is calculated as the share of women with a bank account or loan minus the share of men with a bank account or loan; therefore, a negative differential indicates fewer women are financially included than men, and the smaller (more negative) the differential, the larger the gender gap.

demonstrating that, always and everywhere, women are less included in the financial sector than men at the regional level. The magnitudes of these negative differentials vary considerably between regions; the fact that the Middle East and North Africa (MENA) and South Asia (SA) exhibit the largest gender gaps indicates that cultural factors likely play a role. These regional differences are less marked in the loan-access differentials, where the lower overall access seems to dominate the gender differentiated degree of access. What is most concerning about the data in Table 2.2 is that, for the most part, the gender gaps in financial inclusion have not decreased over time. Even in some of the regions where the gender gap has closed between 2011 and 2017, such as East Asia & Pacific (EAP), there can be observed a reversal in the trend between 2014 and 2017. In other regions, such as Sub-Saharan Africa (SSA), the gender gap has considerably widened over time. Whilst SSA no longer stands out as the worst overall performer in terms of gendered financial inclusion, it does stand out by having the worst relative decline over the sample period. The picture is not improved by consideration of the loan differentials, whereby in all regions bar MENA, the gender gap actually widened between 2011 and 2017. Whilst the role of gender in financial inclusion is already very important for conceptual reasons, as discussed before, results such as these demonstrate the urgency with which gendered financial exclusion must be analyzed and addressed in practical terms. It is in part for this reason that this book contains two full chapters on gender and financial inclusion, and further discussion of these and other results will be held back until then.

In order to dive deeper than regional aggregates, Figure 2.2 presents maps of Africa and Latin America with countries shaded according to the share of adults with a bank account in the latest 2017 round of Findex data. Figure 2.3 presents the same information for developing Asia. High-income countries are excluded, as are countries for which data are not available. For reasons of brevity, we focus on only one of the financial inclusion indicators – share of adults with a bank account – which we acknowledge is insufficient for capturing the *use* element of financial inclusion.[2] The darker the shading, the higher the proportion of adults with a bank account. The patterns that emerge from figures 2.2 and 2.3 give some indication as to which areas in particular exhibit high levels of

---

[2]   Maps of the developing world shaded by the width of the 'gender gap' are presented and discussed in Chapter 4.

financial exclusion. From Figure 2.2, it can be seen that many countries in Central America perform worse in terms of financial inclusion than the major nations of South America, and within South America the Spanish-speaking countries in the west of the continent seem to have fallen behind, especially Colombia and Peru in the north-west. Africa shows relatively high levels of financial inclusion in the more economically successful regions of Southern Africa and East Africa, especially the major countries of the East African Community. By contrast, levels of financial inclusion are shockingly low in the war-ravaged countries of Central Africa, and perhaps surprisingly low in many of the more stable countries of West Africa. With the exception of Libya, levels of FI tend to be low in the Islamic-majority countries, and in general seem to be lower on average in the former French colonies as compared with former British. In general, levels of FI are similar in the more advanced Latin America countries as in the more advanced African countries, but the laggards of Africa are considerably behind those of Latin America. In Central and West Africa, we observe many nations with shares of adults with a bank account below 30%.

Turning to Figure 2.3 we can see that, in much of developing Asia, including many of the largest countries, levels of financial inclusion are quite high. Despite this, there is enormous disparity across the region, with levels in Central Asia and the poorer countries of South-East Asia showing shares of adults with a bank account comparable to the most financially excluded regions of Africa. Islamic countries in Asia are more mixed than in Africa, where Iran has in fact the highest share of adults with a bank account on the continent, and Turkey, Malaysia, and Kazakhstan also perform well. The conflict-ravaged nations of Afghanistan, Iraq, West Bank and Gaza, and Myanmar are the worst performers in the region – similar to the situation in Africa with the lowest levels in many of the unstable nations of Central Africa. One common and unsurprising thread across all three continents is a strong association between the instability and conflict level of a nation and low levels of financial inclusion – from Haiti to Congo, Afghanistan to Sierra Leone, it seems that the disruptions both to tangible infrastructure and intangible social trust brought about by turbulence and conflict severely erode the ability or willingness of citizens to join the formal banking system.[3] These issues will be discussed in greater depth later in this chapter in the section on determinants. Finally, whilst the large swathes of darker shade on the map of Asia may suggest that financial exclusion is a less widespread issue on this continent, it should always be recalled that Asia is vast and the under-banked nations of the Middle East, Central Asia, and South-East Asia still collectively represent tens if not hundreds of millions of people.

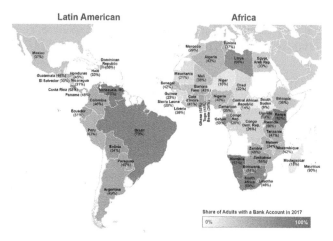

Figure 2.2   2017 levels of financial inclusion in Latin America and Africa

---

[3]   On interesting exception to this is Venezuela, where the share of individuals with a bank account is the second highest in Latin America. As these are 2017 data, it precedes the most severe escalations of civil unrest in that country. It will therefore be very interesting to see the figures for Venezuela in the next round of Findex data – this will tell us a lot about whether enhanced unrest causes people to *detach* from the banking system, or if, once banked initially, people remain banked even in the face of rising conflict levels.

Figure 2.3   2017 levels of financial inclusion in developing Asia

4.   Sub-Saharan Africa and the financial inclusion gap

Financial development and, especially, financial inclusion are important features of the development process in all developing regions. Regional or international comparison can also be of great value in attempting to ascertain why some regions or countries perform so much better than others in terms of their level of financial inclusion. However, many researchers and policymakers within the financial inclusion field choose to focus extensively on Sub-Saharan Africa (SSA), for reasons that will be apparent from the data and discussion presented in the previous section. It was shown in this section that, in most survey years across both measures of financial inclusion, SSA lags significantly behind the other developing regions of the world. This is a common and well-documented finding within both the financial development and financial inclusion literature (Allen et al. 2014), and it can be observed also in the financial development data presented in Chapter 1. It might be thought that this observed lower level of financial inclusion in SSA is a result of the region performing less well than others across other development indicators; for example, SSA also has a lower average income per capita, lower average Human Development Index (HDI) score, etc. This kind of argument fits well with the demand-side approach to theories of the link between finance and development discussed earlier; it would suggest that the reason the level of financial inclusion in SSA is lower than in other developing regions is *because* SSA is poorer on average, and therefore has a lower demand for financial services. Were this the entire story, it would imply that lagging financial inclusion in SSA was not so much of a concern in and of itself, because it is a result of other development variables. However, there are several reasons to dispute this argument.

First, it should be noted that all of the financial development indicators presented were expressed as shares of GDP; this normalization to some extent controls for the differences in national income. Second, the theoretical arguments discussed earlier demonstrate that there is by no means a consensus on a unidirectional causal relationship between financial development and inclusion and economic development and income; the preferred mechanism of bidirectional causality would suggest that SSA performing less well on other development indicators may in part be *as a result of* lower levels of financial development and inclusion, just as the lower levels of financial development and inclusion may in part be due to poor performance in terms of other economic indicators. Third, and most important, a more nuanced examination of the data rules out the possibility that the entire differential between SSA and other developing regions is due to differential levels of economic development. Allen at al. (2014) show that, comparing only SSA countries with countries in other regions at a similar level of development, the SSA countries still perform less well in terms of financial development and inclusion. Similarly, when controlling for all of the major economic variables that may in part drive financial development and inclusion, SSA as a region continues to perform less well than other regions. Clearly, it is insufficient to argue that SSA exhibits lower levels of financial development and financial inclusion than other regions purely because it is less economically developed. This important finding has given rise to the terms *financial development gap* and *financial inclusion gap* to describe the puzzlingly lower levels of financial development and inclusion in SSA as compared with other developing regions. Finding explanations for, and possible solutions to, the financial inclusion gap in SSA is one of the most important tasks for financial inclusion researchers and policymakers, and such findings may have very real and lasting effects on the actual conditions and economies of the world's poorest continent.

5.   Determinants of financial inclusion

In order to improve financial inclusion in general, and to reduce the financial inclusion gap in SSA in particular, it is important to examine which government policies induce financial inclusion, and which individual and country characteristics may explain access to financial markets and intermediaries.

Most 'early' studies on the determinants of financial inclusion focus on country-level proxies. A well-known example is the study by Beck et al. (2007), who examined factors that affect household and small firms' access and use of banking services. The Beck et al. (2007) study is probably most important because of the introduction and reliability of a new set of banking sector outreach indicators, which are used by many to measure financial inclusion, such as the number of branches (ATMs) per $1,000km^2$; the number of branches (ATMs) per 100,000 people; the number of loans (deposits) per 1,000 people and the average size of loans (deposits) per GDP per capita.

In terms of determinants of financial inclusion, Beck et al. (2007) provide some interesting evidence at the country level. Their study suggests positive relationships between financial inclusion variables and GDP per capita, the quality of the overall institutional environment, and the level of infrastructure (measured by telephone lines per capita). The importance of good institutions for financial inclusion had also been emphasized by Honohan (2008), who argued that countries with good institutions of politics or governance are more likely to have increased financial inclusion due to the increased trust in the economy. Good governance, political stability, and quality public services epitomize issues of public accountability that when addressed enhance trust and disclosure. Focus Box 2.2 takes a deeper dive into the historical-institutional roots of contemporary levels of financial inclusion, particularly as related to disparate colonial legacies and legal systems.

It is well known that, for a financial transaction to be successful, trust between both parties of the financial contract is necessary. Lack of trust of one or both parties thus creates an obstacle to extending financial services. In developing countries, lack of trust in the financial system is a major reason that prevents some individuals, households, and businesses from accessing financial services. The lack of trust can stem from previous experiences of bank closures, embezzlement of funds, or political seizures and expropriations and the consequent fear of their reoccurrence. Xu (2020) finds that lack of (social) trust is especially a barrier to financial inclusion for countries with weak formal institutions. Ghosh (2021) shows that trust significantly enhances account ownership and use in India.

Better political institutions also relax legal and contractual process, thus reducing transactions cost. Documentation requirements are often important barriers to financial inclusion. The documents required to, for example, open a bank account or apply for a loan create a barrier in most developing countries where formal identification systems are not widespread. In some cases, financial service providers also ask for alternative documents such as proof of residence, which in themselves are also difficult to access in countries with less formal systems. In such situations individuals and households with no formal documentation are excluded from accessing financial services – a classic example of financial exclusion. Better political institutions, which lower documentation barriers and reduce transaction costs, are therefore key to financial intermediation from a borrower and lender contractual point of view (Nkoa & Song 2020).

It is also argued frequently that information and communications technology (ICT) is instrumental in enhancing financial inclusion (Honohan 2008; Andrianaivo & Kpodar 2011; Ouma et al. 2017). ICT infrastructure can be used to deploy financial services across a wider geographical zone and to reach remote areas at a lower cost. This helps reduce the demand challenges of presence of financial institutions and services. The deployment of branchless banking services such as mobile money, and recently mobile banking is an example of how ICT has helped in dealing with challenges of distance and reducing the transaction cost of extending financial services to individuals and firms that had been previously excluded. People and small businesses with access to mobile money are more likely to be financially included. A related issue is that the widespread access to and use of mobile phones makes it easy to collate information or profile users. This reduced cost of information gathering undoubtedly would reduce the cost of intermediation to financial institutions who are able to tap into ICT infrastructure. Developments in ICT have therefore resulted in a reduced cost of financial intermediation and consequently an increase in financial inclusion. Finally, from a macroeconomic perspective, the presence of unemployment and inequality also hampers financial inclusion in a country (Sarma & Pais 2011). With high unemployment and inequality, a substantial proportion of the population is excluded from income-earning activities.

One of the first studies that exploits individual-level data to examine determinants of financial inclusion is Allen et al. (2016), who use the aforementioned Global Findex Database. They provide an individual-level analysis as well as a country-level analysis. From the individual-level analysis, they find that those who earn higher income, are older, live in urban areas, have higher education, live in smaller households, and are married and employed, are more likely to own an account and frequently use their bank accounts. Surprisingly, they do not find evidence for a significant difference between men and women with respect to account ownership and savings, whilst several other studies suggest considerable gender differences related to financial inclusion. However, the analyses suggest that women are less likely to frequently use an account. Cost of opening and maintaining an account, proximity and bank penetration, information disclosure, legal and political rights, and savings promotion schemes are the most significant drivers of financial inclusion at the country and policy level. The country-level factors show the importance of the architecture of the financial system as a determinant of financial inclusion. Further analysis based on interacting country and policy variables with individual-level variables show that country-level and policy factors that determine financial inclusion are less likely to induce financial inclusion of women and young individuals, as compared with men.

In addition to income, education level, and gender, which are mentioned by several studies (e.g., Zins & Weill 2016) as important, another individual determinant of financial inclusion is financial literacy. Financial literacy is related to education because numeracy skills are key to understanding financial products and services. A financially literate individual or business is an informed agent on the need and use of financial services and will therefore be more likely to be financially included. Furthermore, for financial inclusion to be sustained, people and businesses who access financial services must be informed. Clearly, then, a country with a smaller financially literate population is more likely to experience low levels of financial inclusion. Improving financial literacy may be a useful strategy to bridge the gender gap and the exclusion of the youth in financial services. This is demonstrated in an experimental study by Koomson et al. (2020) on financial literacy in Ghana, where it is found that with financial literacy women and the youth are more likely to be financially included.

Location is also an important determinant of financial inclusion, as in most developing countries financial institutions are centered in a few urban areas, implying that access to finance becomes a challenge for residents who live further away from these centres. For some countries religion also affects financial inclusion. In Islamic finance, for instance, the treatment of interest is different from that of traditional finance and presents a challenge for countries with Muslim residents. In such countries Muslim residents may be less likely to be financially included where Islamic finance is absent.

Following the trends in determinants of financial inclusion, the Global Findex Survey (Demirgüç-Kunt et al. 2017) identifies self-reported barriers to financial inclusion. These are self-reported reasons why individuals are unable to access or own a formal bank account. These barriers include income, distance (the nearest bank being too far away), cost of opening a bank account, lack of required documentation to open an account, lack of trust in the banks, and not enough money to open an account. The barriers also include religious reasons, a household member already having an account, and cases where an individual decides he or she does not need financial services. Interestingly not much progress has been made with respect to some of these barriers over the years. For instance, using data from Global Findex, we observe that there has been a consistent rise in the percentage of adults reporting distance, cost, documentation, trust, and religion as a barrier to financial inclusion. The proportion of adults reporting these barriers has almost doubled since 2011 for most of the barriers and quadrupled in the case of trust.

Focus box 2.2   **Institutions and legal codes: deep determinants of financial inclusion**

In the field of economic development, many leading researchers have focused on tracing the deep roots of current development conditions in the historical and institutional origins of regions and countries, often with fascinating results (North 1990; Acemoglu et al. 2001). One of the most distinct and persistent institutional features of a country is its legal system. The influence of differences in legal systems and legal institutional origins on present-day development outcomes was emphasized and explored by Levine (1998), based in turn on the differential impacts of common vs. civil law legal systems on contemporary contract protection uncovered by La Porta et al. (1998). This historical–legal–institutional framework was then applied to financial sectors in two important papers by Beck et al. (2003a, 2003b), which propose that these differences in foundational legal systems still act as a core determinant of developing country financial sector performance and development to this day, and attempt to unpick the mechanisms by which this occurs.

The basis of the argument is that most developing countries, and almost all Sub-Saharan African countries, can be said to fall into one of two legal traditions – common law or civil law.[4] Which of these legal systems a country adopted is broadly a product of historical happenstance – most commonly colonial history – but, once adopted, these systems become extraordinarily persistent and path dependent (La Porta et al. 1998; Beck et al. 2003a). The general difference between the two legal systems is that common law involves decision-making through a process of legal precedent, whereas civil law is codified. Common law derived from 12th-century England, whereas civil law evolved from Roman law via Napoleonic France (Yermack 2018). Therefore, former British colonies tend to be founded in common law, whereas former French (and Belgian) colonies tend to be founded in civil law – with much of Sub-Saharan Africa having fallen into one of these two empires. The principal differences from the perspective of strength of contract enforcement and robustness against expropriation are twofold: (1) because common law is based on precedent, it is inherently predictable in terms of application and interpretation, and (2) because common law allows cases to be initiated by private plaintiffs, contracting parties have direct recourse to the law when they feel their

---

[4]   La Porta et al. (1998) actually distinguish between four legal systems: British (common), French (civil), German, and Scandinavian – the latter two of which can be thought somewhat as hybrids of common and civil. As the literature has evolved into explaining a broader range of outcomes, however, the focus has shifted more towards the dichotomy of common vs civil law (La Porta et al. 2000; Yermack 2018), with either German and French law aggregated together, or German and Scandinavian law used as intermediary positions to emphasize the dichotomy on either side.

rights have been violated. Civil law, by contrast, is written by legal theorists and academics in the form of legal codes that are often untested until they are first applied, and requires civil or public authorities to initiate litigation. Both of these differences result in contractors in common law countries feeling more secure and protected in terms of their contractual rights, as La Porta et al. (1998) argue and empirically demonstrate.

The theoretical steps from legal institutions to protection of contractual rights to financial development and inclusion may then seem fairly natural – if one legal system ensures better protection of financial contracts, it is likely that *ceteris paribus* more such contracts will be entered into in countries with this legal system, and that the financial system will therefore become larger and broader. However, as Beck et al. (2003b) note, the precise mechanisms by which legal institutional tradition determine modern day financial development are not quite so clear-cut *a priori*. Two alternative mechanisms are proposed and subjected to empirical testing – a political channel, by which common law leads to greater protection of private property rights via its emphasis on the centrality of the individual rather than the state, and an adaptability channel, by which common law as a result of its basis in legal precedent and interpretation adapts more quickly and efficiently to new socioeconomic conditions, technologies, and contexts. Beck et al. (2003b) test these mechanisms by developing indicators for both channels instrumented by the national legal traditions and then testing the econometric explanatory power of these indicators on various aspects of financial development such as volume of private credit or level of stock market development. They conclude that the adaptability channel is the more relevant one in linking legal origin to modern day level of financial development.

Beck et al. (2003a, 2003b) precede the shift in focus from financial development to financial inclusion as documented in Chapter 1; however, it is easy to speculate as to how institutional origins may influence modern-day financial inclusion via similar channels – essentially, it is through trust in and predictability of the contractual and legal landscapes that the impacts manifest, and, as was discussed in the body of this chapter, lack of trust in institutions is a key driver of financial exclusion. Yermack (2018) shows that the disparity in financial development indicators between common and civil law countries in Sub-Saharan Africa also holds for financial inclusion indicators, again with common law countries enjoying considerably higher levels of financial inclusion. Precise causal identification of the effects of such long-run macroeconomic indicators is of course very difficult, and one could speculate that to an extent these legal origins proxy for numerous other fundamental latent variables. Nevertheless, regardless of the precise relative importance of competing mechanisms, this disparity between common and civil law developing countries is clearly an empirical reality, and acknowledging and understanding it is certainly an important part of understanding what determines financial development and inclusion outcomes in the very, very long run.

6.   Summary and future

This chapter has paid attention to some key concepts of financial inclusion. It has also presented some important figures on financial inclusion for different regions in the world, and drawn attention to financial inclusion for Sub-Saharan Africa. Most importantly, it has discussed country-level and individual factors that drive financial inclusion, which help to explain why some countries exhibit higher levels of financial inclusion than others even when similar across other indicators, and why there is such a financial inclusion gap between Sub-Saharan Africa and the rest of the developing world. Now that these underlying drivers are better understood, we need to develop workable policy prescriptions and development policy tools and programs so as to boost financial inclusion across the developing world, and in particular to close financial inclusion gaps. It is also of paramount importance to ensure that such gains in financial inclusion are inclusive across gender and other minority groups. It is equally essential to utilize rigorous tools of evaluation to ensure that such policies achieve the desired effects on financial inclusion, do not generate harmful side-effects, and are efficient in terms of the cost–benefit tradeoff – in particular, experimental research in the form of randomized controlled trials (RCTs) can help to perform such evaluations. The forthcoming chapters of this book will lay out in detail the current state of play in the literature with regards to these fundamental challenges; however, there is still so much to be done that the interested reader may already begin to speculate about the future of research into financial inclusion in developing countries, and what contribution they may aspire to make.

3. Impacts of financial inclusion

1. Introduction

In 2005 the United Nations Economic and Social Council launched the Year of Microcredit to build support for making financial services more accessible to poor and low-income people. The main goal was to ensure that poor people would get more access to financial services, like credit, savings, insurance, transfers, and remittances. The importance of building inclusive financial sectors was emphasized by many policymakers and academics, amongst others by Kofi Annan, the UN Secretary-General at that time, who argued, "The great challenge before us is to address the constraints that exclude people from full participation in the financial sector. Together, we can and must build inclusive financial sectors that help people improve their lives."[1]

The striving to improve access to finance for poor people seems successful, at the least to some extent. As was shown in Chapter 2, the share of individuals with a bank account increased enormously in the 2011–2017 period. We have also seen a steady growth of the amount of microfinance programs that serve poor people, from 655 in 1997 to more than 10,000 in 2016 (Lensink and Bulte, 2019). However, an increase in financial inclusion does not automatically imply a reduction in poverty. At the beginning of the 21st century, supported by an enormous number of anecdotes and simple empirical analyses, there was an almost euphoric attitude amongst policymakers about the potentially positive impacts of providing access to (micro) finance to the poor. It was even argued that poverty would

---

[1]   At https://www.yearofmicrocredit.org/#.

automatically decline if the poor were to get access to finance, especially credit. More recently several academics have started to cast doubts about what could be achieved by simply enhancing financial access to the poor. In fact, the question whether providing access to finance to poor people had a positive impact has divided the academic community, not the least because measuring impact is notoriously difficult.

This chapter aims to discuss the literature on the impact of financial inclusion. We start, in Section 2, by providing a theoretical analysis of the channels by which financial inclusion could impact the poor. Next, we will turn to empirical studies, starting with the broad literature on the impact of microfinance, in Section 3. Section 4 discusses the impacts of government and banking interventions, after which we resort to the literature on the impact of financial inclusion at the macro level.

2.   Theory and expectations

At the most general level, some of the reasons why we may expect increases in financial inclusion to have impacts both at the individual and societal levels have been touched upon in Chapter 1 – a larger and more developed financial sector can help facilitate capital investments and reduce financial frictions such that growth opportunities can be maximized, both by individual enterprises and by countries, and a more inclusive financial system can help to ensure these opportunities are distributed more equitably (Abor et al. 2021). At the level of individuals, the ability to relax liquidity constraints and intertemporally reallocate resources via saving and borrowing increases their choice sets and their ability to better accommodate their own risk preferences, and provides the opportunity to overcome hurdles to entrepreneurial activity and the development of microenterprises. There can of course be negative individual level effects also, particularly in the realm of credit access and usage, if people take on too much debt or do not use borrowed money responsibly; this problem is exacerbated in situations when the cost of credit is usurious.

To better understand the theory and expectations of the impacts of financial inclusion, and to motivate the empirical research that will be discussed extensively in the remainder of this chapter, it is useful to be more systematic in the presentation and categorization of theoretical mechanisms. We take as a basis for this the Financial Inclusion 'Theory of Change' diagram proposed by Duvendack & Mader (2020). An adjusted version of this figure is replicated here, as Figure 3.1.

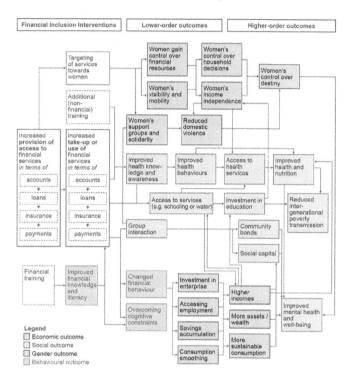

Figure 3.1   Theoretical outcomes of financial inclusion interventions

In Figure 3.1, Duvendack & Mader (2020) organize the theories of the impacts of financial inclusion at the individual/household level along a number of dimensions. First, they identify four categories of *outcomes* that we might on the basis of theory expect to be influenced by financial inclusion. These are *economic* outcomes, *gender* outcomes, *behavioural* outcomes, and *social* outcomes. Dividing outcomes in this way is useful both because it helps to isolate the purposes of different FI interventions and guide the selection of indicators for impact evaluation, and also because it acts as a reminder that traditional economic outcomes are just one way in which FI can impact recipients. In addition, theoretical impacts are divided into 'lower-order' and 'higher-order' outcomes. The term lower-order outcomes refers to the immediate and direct impacts of financial inclusion, while higher-order outcomes refers to the more entrenched, wider impacts of these direct effects. For example, access to an actuarially fair crop insurance product might yield the lower-order outcome of smoother average incomes around harvest time, and the higher-order outcome of investments in riskier and more profitable crops and more mature attitudes to risk management. As with all program and policy evaluations, it is more difficult to measure impacts on higher-order than on lower-order outcomes, not least because the former can take more time to manifest. The theoretical links through to higher-order outcomes are also often more ambiguous. At the same time, it is these higher-order outcomes that are seen as truly transformative. The inputs into Duvendack & Mader's schema are then the different types of financial inclusion intervention, which are themselves motivated by FI initiatives that identify gaps in the existing landscape.

The four categories of outcomes are arranged as follows. *Economic outcomes* include intensive margin effects on household income, consumption and consumption smoothing, microenterprise profits, and savings, as well as extensive margin effects such as influencing the decision to launch a microenterprise or undertake a risky investment. Different financial inclusion interventions might be expected to influence these economic outcomes in different ways; for example, access to and usage of credit may relax liquidity constraints and facilitate optimal intertemporal reallocation of resources, access to secure savings facilities may allow for saving towards investments or asset purchases, access to insurance products may facilitate riskier investments, etc. The formal theory behind these mechanisms often mirrors established macroeconomic theory in developed country contexts, for example the Fisher model for intertemporal optimization of consumption with savings and liquidity constraints (Fisher 1930; Zeldes 1989; Deaton 1991); or the model of Holtz-Eakin et al. (1994) for the impact of liquidity constraints on entrepreneurial income and survival. In terms of higher-order economic outcomes, these may include the generation of sustainable income streams, the ability to afford more education for children and family members, the creation of new jobs in the expanding microenterprises, etc.

Next, *gender outcomes* involve the extent to which financial inclusion and FI interventions have differential impacts for women as for men, not just in terms of economic and equality benefits and closing the 'gender gap', but also in positively impacting women empowerment. Chapters 4 and 5 provide an extensive overview of the gender dimension of FI and FI interventions; as such all discussion of theory of, and impacts on, gender outcomes is held back until then. *Behavioural outcomes* take into account the theory and empirical finding that financial services can lead to cognitive and behavioural changes. For example, money-usage patterns, attitudes to risk, degree of myopia, and rationality of decision-making may all be impacted by the availability of, and accumulated experience of, using a wider and more sophisticated range of financial products and services. Duvendack & Mader treat these all as lower-order outcomes as they mostly contain only the potential for more tangible knock-on effects; however, it could be argued that permanent adjustments in behaviours and attitudes that aggregate to the societal level do indeed represent higher-order outcomes.

The term *social outcomes* is used by Duvendack & Mader as a 'catch-all' category for beneficial outcomes that do not fall strictly under the other three categories. Specifically, this includes but is not limited to health outcomes, social-relational outcomes, and access to services. The primary mechanism linking financial inclusion to health outcomes is fairly straightforward: the ability to save or borrow expands the range of medicines and health services that can be accessed in countries where quality public provision of these is not widespread. Dupas and Robinson (2013a) uncover a large latent demand for specific health savings facilities amongst informal savings club members in Kenya. The economic outcomes discussed above, such as increased incomes and consumption, could also lead to improvements in nutrition with concomitant health implications, especially when involving the nutrition of children. This primary mechanism can also be supplemented by health trainings and information sessions delivered alongside the FI intervention when it is specifically targeted at health incomes. Similar mechanisms would guide the route from financial inclusion to accessing other services such as education, social care, etc. The social-relational outcomes are a little more complicated as they are guided as much by the *participation* in financial inclusion programs and the business opportunities they hopefully provide, with the networking and community-building effects of such participation, as by the economic outcomes themselves. Similar mechanisms underpin the *societal empowerment* element of the gender and women empowerment impacts of financial inclusion.

Figure 3.1 traces the stages through which different financial inclusion interventions may be expected to lead to the different lower- and then higher-order outcomes. It can be noted that different types of outcomes feed into each other, and certain lower-order outcomes are prerequisites for those further up the chain. The core economic outcomes of investments in enterprises, employment opportunities, savings accumulation, and consumption smoothing first require behavioural outcomes in terms of financial behaviour, and these in turn lead to some social and gender outcomes. However, it can also be seen from the upper half of the figure that key social and gender outcomes can be impacted even when bypassing the core economic outcomes, either as a result of interaction and community effects or empowerment effects; and that therefore even financial inclusion interventions that do not have detectable economic impacts may still lead to these other desirable outcomes. Indeed, many may be specifically designed to target and prioritize these outcomes.

3.   Impacts of microfinance

The primary policy tool aimed at boosting financial inclusion in developing countries remains microfinance. Already introduced in previous chapters, microfinance products and services can, and often are, offered by private microfinance banks, but also form the backbone of many financial inclusion interventions by NGOs and international development organizations, either in partnership with existing private sector banks, or as separate entities. It is also through microfinance interventions that much of the rigorous *empirical evidence* regarding the impacts of financial inclusion is ascertained; as these interventions are administered directly by international development actors and researchers, impact evaluations can be designed and performed alongside the interventions in the form of randomized controlled trials (RCTs).

The challenge in any impact evaluation is to isolate the causal effect of the intervention from other determinants of wellbeing, so-called confounders. When comparing households with and without microcredit, the observed difference may not solely be attributed to the loan obtained from the MFI. There may, for instance, be a change in tax policies during the time of the intervention that potentially affects income of the respondents, such that comparing households before and after the intervention will measure not only the impact of the intervention but also the change in tax policies. Moreover, households who are allowed to borrow from MFIs may be poorer than households who are not allowed to borrow from MFIs even before they got access to microfinance, such that a simple comparison of households with and without access to microfinance measures not only the impact of (access to) microfinance but also the effect of being poorer before the intervention started. It may also be the case that only very innovative households decide to borrow from a microfinance organization (*self-selection bias*), while seemingly similar households who are less innovative decide not to borrow. Once again, a simple comparison of households with and without microfinance will not measure the impact of microfinance, but a combination of impact of microfinance and impact of being innovative. Finally, the MFI may deliberately decide to open branches in regions with better infrastructure, leading to so-called *program placement bias*, which also implies that a simple comparison of households with and without microfinance will not measure the impact of microfinance.

The preferred approach to overcome the abovementioned biases is to conduct a RCT. The RCT approach assigns (groups) of households to treatment and control groups by lottery, such that, in theory, the only difference between both groups is due to the (microfinance) intervention. These evaluations both provide evidence related to the efficacy of the specific microfinance intervention and add to the body of evidence regarding the impacts of financial inclusion in general. It should, however, always be remembered that these are a *specific type* of financial inclusion; so, for example, the impacts of access to microfinance credit or microfinance savings accounts may not necessarily be homogenous with the impacts of improved access to credit or savings more generally. Nevertheless, as most people in developing countries will only be borrowing or saving in small amounts anyway, the impacts of changes in financial inclusion driven by microfinance likely form a useful guide as to the effects of changes in financial inclusion more generally, at least at the individual or household level.

A limitation of most impact analysis is that they usually capture only *partial equilibrium effects*. That is, only the *direct effect* of the intervention on the individuals or households that receive it is captured, as compared with those who do not receive the intervention.[2] *General equilibrium effects*, such as feedback effects or spillovers to other markets or to the entire local economy, are generally not captured. Therefore, if increases in financial inclusion have additional benefits beyond the direct recipients, such as raising the amount of money that is spent in local businesses, the analysis will underestimate the positive impacts; if, on the other hand, increases in financial inclusion have negative side effects, such as crowding out informal savings clubs and the networking benefits they bring, the analysis will overestimate the positive impacts.

For a long time, policymakers had to make do with almost exclusively such partial equilibrium evidence for the evaluation of financial inclusion programs. However, a hugely important recent paper by Breza & Kinnan (2021) has changed that, providing high-quality evidence for the general equilibrium impacts of microfinance in the context of India. Therefore, Section 3.1 will discuss the body of RCT evidence for the partial equilibrium impacts of financial inclusion driven by microfinance interventions, then Section 3.2 will discuss the general equilibrium impacts as established by Breza & Kinnan and some earlier, non-RCT papers. Additionally, this section on the impacts of microfinance, in addition to the sections on microfinance and gender in Chapter 5, focuses for the most part on *credit* and *savings* products, and not so much on *insurance*. However, as insurance is also an important and under-available financial product in developing countries, focus boxes 3.1 and 3.2 delve a little deeper into the theory and empirics of the impacts of insurance products.

Focus box 3.1   Insurance: relevance; index insurance and bundled insurance products

The financial inclusion literature in general, and the microfinance literature in particular is paying increasingly greater attention to the importance of access to insurance products. The reason is simple. Poor people often must cope with very variable incomes. This especially holds

---

[2]   Although some cleverly designed RCTs are able to incorporate and quantitatively estimate the *externalities* caused by policy interventions by adding additional comparison groups; the classic example is Miguel & Kremer (2004), who show that providing deworming tablets to schoolchildren has additional benefits even for those who do not receive the tablets, but are in classrooms with those who do.

for smallholder farmers who face huge fluctuations in farming yields because of weather variation, diseases, pests, etc. There is increasing evidence that high risk is an important factor impeding the uptake of new agricultural technologies, such as improved crop varieties and fertilizers, which are important to improve the performance of the agricultural sector.

Insurance products would help to reduce risk, and therefore in theory could be beneficial for risk-averse farmers, and help to increase the use of modern technologies. A simple example can explain this. Assume that there are two risk-averse farmers (A and B), who produce the same crop and use the same amounts of land and other inputs. There are two possibilities: (1) there is a good harvest that yields $2000, and (2) there is a bad harvest, which yields $1000. Assume that the probability of a good harvest is 0.5.

If there is no mutual insurance, the following four possibilities for farmer A result:

1. Farmer A will experience a good harvest, and so does farmer B. The probability that this happens equals $0.5 \times 0.5 = 0.25$. In this case farmer A will obtain $2000.
2. Farmer A will experience a bad harvest, and so does farmer B. The probability that this happens also equals 0.25. In this case farmer A will gain $1000.
3. Farmer A experiences a good harvest, while farmer B experiences a bad harvest. Again, the probability of this event is 0.25 and farmer A will gain $2000.
4. Farmer B experiences a good harvest, while farmer A experiences a bad harvest. The probability of this event again equals 0.25. Farmer A will then receive ($1000).

The above implies that the expected income for farmer A, without insurance, will equal: $0.25 \times 2000 + 0.25 \times 1000 + 0.25 \times 2000 + 0.25 \times 1000 = 1500$.

Next, we consider what happens in case of mutual insurance. Assume that farmer A will pay $500 to farmer B in case farmer A experiences a good harvest and farmer B experiences a bad harvest. Moreover, farmer B will pay $500 to farmer A if farmer B experiences good harvest and farmer A bad harvest. Again, there are four possibilities, but now the expected income calculation for farmer A will differ as a farmer who experiences good weather will transfer some money to a farmer experiencing bad weather: $0.25 \times 2000 + 0.25 \times 1000 + 0.25 \times 1500 +$

$0.25 \times 1500 = 1500$.

The effect of mutual insurance is straightforward: while expected income doesn't change, the variability of the income stream becomes smaller in the cases where one of the two farmers experiences a bad harvest while the other farmer experiences a good harvest, an income transfer between the two farmers will take place. Therefore, for a risk-averse farmer confronted with variable income streams, access to a (mutual) insurance product can be beneficial, which may induce farmers to increase investments and use (risky) modern agricultural technologies. Indeed, Cai et al. (2015) and Liu et al. (2020) provide evidence for investment enhancing effects of insurance. However, in practice the availability and uptake of insurance products by smallholders appears to be very small.

One important reason for low uptake is a shortage of liquid funds. Insurance products typically need to be bought during the planting season, when farmers are liquidity constraint. Focus Box 3.2 presents a theoretical model showing that allowing farmers to pay the premium payment later may induce a substantial increase in uptake.

The availability may be low because insurance systems will only work if the different outcome possibilities are independent: insuring risks due to weather shocks can be difficult as very often all farmers in a village are affected similarly by bad weather (covariate risk), so that outputs are highly correlated. Moreover, indemnity-based mutual insurance systems suffer from moral hazard and adverse selection problems, which make insurance companies reluctant to offer insurance products to farmers in remote areas.

In order to come around adverse selection and moral hazard problems insurance companies started to experiment with *index-insurance* products. Index-insurance delinks payouts from individual farmer behaviours, by triggering payouts when an objectively quantifiable and verifiable index – for instance a measure of local rainfall during a certain period – differs from a pre-determined threshold. Hill et al. (2019) is one of the few studies that considers the impact of index insurance. They show, for example, using a randomized field experiment in Bangladesh, that index insurance induced farmers to invest more in risk-increasing agricultural inputs.

However, index-based insurance may suffer from *basis risk*. This means it provides only imperfect coverage for shocks if individual damages are not perfectly correlated with the index, for example if rainfall around the measurement station is sufficient, while this is not the case at the plot of the farmer, which partly explains the low uptake of index insurance.

Due to the low adoption of stand-alone indemnity and index-insurance products, various organizations started to bundle insurance with other financial and non-financial services, such as with loans and access to agricultural inputs. An interlinked insurance–credit–input system in theory could be beneficial for all parties involved. However, rigorous empirical evidence is very scarce, with conflicting results. Karlan et al. (2014) compare the impacts of capital grants, insurance, and their combination, and show that risk is the binding constraint on farmers, not credit. They conclude, "the lesson should not be to simply bundle rainfall insurance with loans but to use the delivery infrastructure and perhaps the trust that microfinance institutions or banks may have in the community to market and distribute rainfall insurance" (Karlan et al. 2014, 648). Bulte et al. (2020) study the relevance of bundling insurance with inputs, and find that providing free insurance increases the adoption of modern technologies. Belissa et al. (2021) find that, in contrast to standalone insurance, a package consisting of insurance, credit, and inputs significantly increases investments in modern agricultural technologies, which confirms the relevance of bundled insurance products.

Focus box 3.2   The importance of delaying premium payments

Below we will show with a theoretical model that delaying the payment of the insurance premium may help to enhance uptake.[3]

We assume that there is a continuum of farmers indexed by their current available stock of liquidity y_0, $y_0 \epsilon \left[y_0^L, y_0^H \right]$, with $y_0^H > y_0^L \geq 0$. The measure of all farmers is normalized to unity and has the cumulative distribution denoted F, with $0 \leq F\left(y_0^L\right) < F\left(y_0^H\right) = 1$, where $F\left(y\right)$ is the proportion of farmers with liquidity less than (or equal to) y. There are two periods,

---

[3]   The model is drawn from Belissa et al. (2020).

$t = 0,1$. There is no uncertainty at $t = 0$, but outcomes in $t = 1$ are uncertain. The farmer has a certain amount of liquidity y_0 in period 0 and an uncertain income $\tilde{y}_1$ in period 1. Period 1 income is positively dependent on rainfall, which is stochastic. The farmer's two-period utility without insurance is given by:

$$\underline{U} \equiv u\left(y_0\right) + \beta\left[\bar{y}_1 - \left(\tfrac{1}{2}\right)\rho\sigma_y^{\;2}\right] \quad (1)$$

where, $\bar{y}_1 \equiv E\left(\tilde{y}_1\right)$, $\sigma_y^{\;2}$ is the variance of $\tilde{y}_1$, β represents time-preference, ρ is the farmer's constant absolute risk-aversion parameter, and E is the expectations operator.

Assumption 1: We assume that $u'(.) > 0$, $u''(.) < 0$ and that $u(.)$ satisfies the Inada end-point conditions. The farmer is risk averse and this is represented by a second period utility function that can be expressed in certainty-equivalent form.

The farmer can buy a rainfall-indexed insurance contract that pays out depending on rainfall realizations. The insurance pay-out, $\tilde{x}$, is inversely dependent on rainfall and given that $\tilde{y}$ is positively correlated with rainfall we have $\tilde{x}$ and $\tilde{y}$ negatively correlated – that is, $Cov\left(\tilde{x}, \tilde{y}_1\right) \equiv \sigma_{xy} < 0$. Let the cost (or premium) for this insurance be denoted π, $\bar{x} \equiv E\left(\tilde{x}\right)$ and $\sigma_x^{\;2}$ is the variance of $\tilde{x}$. The farmer has two options: (i) to stay without insurance and have a two-period utility given by (1); or, (ii) buy insurance and obtain a two-period utility given by equation (2) below. Buying insurance entitles the farmer to an income stream $\tilde{z} \equiv \tilde{y}_1 + \tilde{x}$ in period 1. If the farmer buys insurance, she gets:[4]

$$U^0 = u\left(y_0 - \pi\right) + \beta\left[\bar{y}_1 + \bar{x} - \left(\tfrac{1}{2}\right)\rho\left(\sigma_y^{\;2} + \sigma_x^{\;2} + 2\sigma_{xy}\right)\right]$$

---

[4]   This results from the fact that the variance of the sum of two random variables, equals the variance of variable 1, plus the variance of variable 2, plus two time the covariance, that is, Var(x+y) = var(x) + var(y) + 2cov(x,y).

$$\cong u\left(y_0\right)-\pi u'\left(y_0\right)+\beta\left[\bar{y}_1+\bar{x}-\left(\tfrac{1}{2}\right)\rho\left(\sigma_y^{\,2}+\sigma_x^{\,2}+2\sigma_{xy}\right)\right]$$

(2)

where we have used a first-order Taylor expansion to derive the expression in the second line of (2). The farmer buys insurance if and only if equation (2) utility is greater than $\underline{U}$, that is, if

$$\beta\left[\bar{x}-\left(\tfrac{1}{2}\right)\rho\left(\sigma_x^{\,2}+2\sigma_{xy}\right)\right]\geq\pi u'\left(y_0\right). \quad (3)$$

The left-hand side (LHS) of inequality (3) is the additional utility from buying into the uncertain income stream generated by insurance – that is, insurance reduces risk and hence increases utility for a risk-averse smallholder. The right-hand side (RHS) is the utility cost of buying the income stream generated by insurance – that is, the insurance premium π multiplied by the (marginal) cost of liquidity $u'\left(y_0\right)$. While the benefits from insurance will accrue in the next period, and only if rainfall is low, the premium has to be paid today. The relative comparison of cost and benefit depends on the premium, π, but also on the utility cost for the farmer who loses liquidity today. The same premium will mean different things to different farmers, depending on the amount of liquidity they have today. We measure this cost of liquidity by $u'\left(y_0\right)$ with the implicit assumption that, as y_0 rises, the cost of liquidity falls. Observe that, if $u'\left(y_0\right)=1$, the RHS of (3) is simply the premium, or the benefit of insurance must be greater than its premium. As y_0 decreases, $u'\left(.\right)$ falls, implying that people with smaller period 0 liquidity will suffer a greater utility cost of paying the insurance premium.[5] Given insurance pay-out $\tilde{x}$, let (3) hold with equality at $y_0=y^*$. Then all farmers with $y_0\geq y^*$ will buy insurance and others will not buy the insurance. Hence, the proportion of farmers buying

---

[5] This cost of liquidity in period 0 will depend on a number of different factors in addition to income – size of the family, outstanding debt obligations that are payable today, cost of education of children, etc. For simplicity, we assume income is a sufficient measure of liquidity cost.

insurance equals $1 - F\left(y^*\right)$. The analysis so far shows that weather insurance is only beneficial for relatively 'rich' farmers, who have enough possibilities to obtain funds to pay for the insurance premium upfront – that is, for those farmers for whom liquidity costs are not too high. Indeed, uptake of insurance products by smallholders is in practice often very low.

Belissa et al. (2019), Casaburi & Willis (2018), and Liu et al. (2020), establish that the uptake of (weather) insurance products will increase substantially if premium payments are postponed. Below we will explain formally why this may be the case.

Suppose the farmer has access to another insurance product, which we call an IOU, with the same pay-out plan as the erstwhile insurance, but its premium can be paid in the second period. The delayed premium payment is of an amount $\pi\left(1+r\right)$ where r is the risk-free interest rate that the insurance company could get on its one-period cash holdings. If the farmer takes this, she gets utility:

$$U^I = u\left(y_0\right) + \beta\left[\bar{y}_1 + \bar{x} - \pi\left(1+r\right) - \left(\tfrac{1}{2}\right)\rho\left(\sigma_y^2 + \sigma_x^2 + 2\sigma_{xy}\right)\right] \quad (4)$$

Observe that the two-period utility in (4) will be greater than that in (1) if and only if

$$\beta\left[\bar{x} - \left(\tfrac{1}{2}\right)\rho\left(\sigma_x^2 + 2\sigma_{xy}\right)\right] \geq \pi\beta\left(1+r\right) \quad (5)$$

There may exist a subsample of farmers who will buy the IOU if offered, even if they do not buy the standard insurance. In particular, farmers with high liquidity cost will not buy the standard insurance, but some of them will buy the IOU if offered. Theoretically, in a perfect capital market, identical rates of time discount, no aggregate uncertainty and with a borrowing rate equal to the lending rate, the rate of time discount will be such that $\beta\left(1+r\right) = 1$ and the RHS of (5) collapses to π. This is the same as the RHS of (3) when $u'\left(y_0\right) = 1$. The question then boils down to the relative sizes of $\beta\left(1+r\right)$ and $u'\left(y_0\right)$ and that of $\beta\left[\bar{x} - \left(\tfrac{1}{2}\right)\rho\left(\sigma_x^2 + 2\sigma_{xy}\right)\right]$ and π.

One possibility is depicted in Figure 3.2. On the horizontal axis we measure today's non-stochastic income, and the vertical axis measures the money value of utility. Given our assumption of decreasing utility costs of liquidity in income, we obtain the falling $\pi u'(y_0)$ line. By construction, $\beta\left[\bar{x}-\left(\frac{1}{2}\right)\rho\left(\sigma_x^2+2\sigma_{xy}\right)\right]\geq\pi u'(y_0)$ for all $y\geq y^*$ and hence $\left[1-F\left(y^*\right)\right]$ proportion of farmers will buy the standard insurance while $F\left(y^*\right)$ will not buy anything.

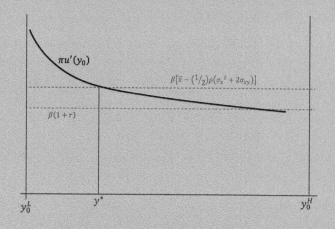

Figure 3.2   Model of insurance markets under seasonal liquidity constraints

To complete the analysis we consider the firm selling insurance. Since all buyers of insurance (and the IOU) get paid according to a rainfall index, all farmers face the same probability of receiving a payout. From Figure 3.2, we know the proportion of farmers who buy the standard insurance, namely $\left[1-F\left(y^*\right)\right]$. Suppose this translates to $N\left(y^*\right)$ farmers, with $N'\left(y^*\right)<0$. If the insurance company makes non-negative profit, its expected pay-out must be less than its expected receipt of premium:

$$N\left(y^*\right)\bar{x}\leq N\left(y^*\right)\pi\left(1+r\right) \text{ or, } \bar{x}\leq\pi\left(1+r\right) \qquad (6)$$

Here we assume that the premium paid in period 0 is held by the insurance company as a risk-less interest-bearing asset. For the insurance market to work, both equations (3) and (6) must be satisfied – that is, for a given rain-indexed schedule of pay-outs $\tilde{x}$, there exists $y^* \epsilon \left[y_0^L, y_0^H \right)$ and $\pi \epsilon \left(0, \infty \right)$ such that both (3) and (6) are satisfied.

In the IOU, the premium payment is deferred to period 1 and the relevant expressions are (5) and (6). If we assume that there is no default – that is, all farmers pay $\pi \left(1 + r \right)$ if they sign up for the IOU, then equation (6) remains the same as long as π is the same in the IOU as it was in the standard insurance. And for (5) and (6) both to hold we need:

$$\left[\bar{x} - \left(\frac{1}{2} \right) \rho \left(\sigma_x^2 + 2 \sigma_{xy} \right) \right] \geq \pi \left(1 + r \right) \geq \bar{x} \quad (7)$$

Hence, for insurance to be sustainable we must have $\left(\sigma_x^2 + 2 \sigma_{xy} \right) < 0$; otherwise, the provider of insurance will make a loss.[6] Assuming this is the case, we can show two results. First, all risk-averse farmers will prefer the IOU over the standard product. Second, all farmers will purchase insurance via the IOU if that is offered to them. Both results are clear from Figure 3.2.

---

[6]   In fact, the following two assumptions need to be satisfied: (a) insurance payout and farmer's income are negatively correlated ($2 \sigma_{xy} < 0$), and (b) pay-outs must be such that $\left(\sigma_x^2 + 2 \sigma_{xy} \right) < 0$. Obviously, if (b) is satisfied, so is (a) (since $\sigma_x^2 > 0$). The probability that these are satisfied improves as the correlation between the rainfall index and the farmer's income (from farming) improves. If the rainfall index is perfectly (positively) correlated with the farmer's income, that is, the index used is the amount of rainfall on the farmer's land, then there is no basis risk for the farmer. But if the index is based in measurement of rain elsewhere, the correlation may not be perfect.

3.1 Partial equilibrium effects

Prior to the advent of the use of RCTs for evaluating microfinance interventions, early studies utilized mostly non-experimental evidence and often relied on surveys and self-reporting of the efficacy of microfinance by the recipients. Such studies were subject to severe biases related to reporting issues, selection issues, and placement issues. Yet, a few exceptions are notable, such as the highly cited study by Pitt and Khandker (1998), who used a quasi-experimental survey design intended to mitigate the aforementioned biases; these authors found large positive marginal impacts of microcredit on household consumption and assets, particularly for women and for poorer households. However, even this paper was subject to severe later criticism by Chemin (2008), Duvendack & Palmer-Jones (2011), and Roodman & Morduch (2014), who all point out methodological issues and find negligible impacts when they attempt to replicate the paper, arguing that the original results were driven exclusively by outliers and flawed econometric assumptions. Roodman & Morduch (2014) conclude that their replication "raises a broad question about the value of non-randomised studies", and that, for non-experimental research to be of any value in supplementing RCTs, "the quality of the natural experiments must be high, and demonstrated." It is likely for these reasons that, since the early 2000s, partial equilibrium analyses of the impacts of microfinance have been dominated by RCTs.[7]

The total number of RCTs evaluating the impacts of microfinance now runs into the hundreds, with most focusing predominantly on the

---

[7] A counter argument, which emphasizes the importance of natural experiments and theoretical research in complementing controlled experiments, can be found in Deaton & Cartwright (2018), who argue, "RCTs can play a role in building scientific knowledge and useful predictions but they can only do so as part of a cumulative program, combining with other methods, including conceptual and theoretical development." The core messages of both Roodman & Morduch (2014) and Deaton & Cartwright (2018) are not contradictory: both call for an appropriate mix of experimental and non-experimental evidence, and for a high degree of rigor to be applied to both. However, in practice a period of a complete lack of experimental evidence in the 1990s probably was followed by an overreliance on experimental evidence in the 2000s, as can be seen by the dominance of RCT evidence in Section 3.1. Fortunately, recent studies such as Breza & Kinnan (2021) seem to indicate a move towards the kind of evidence-mix that both Roodman & Morduch and Deaton & Cartwright consider optimal.

provision of credit (Hermes & Lensink 2021). Addressing all individual RCTs within this chapter is therefore impossible.[8] Even the total number of meta-analyses, surveys, reviews, and reviews of reviews are becoming so large as to prevent a full overview. All this is to the good, however, as a large and geographically diffuse body of work helps to overcome some of the accusations of RCTs being overly context-specific or insufficiently generalizable. The body of surveys and reviews includes Armendariz & Morduch (2010), Bauchet et al. (2011), Duvendack et al. (2011), Van Rooyen et al. (2012), Banerjee et al. (2015b), Hermes & Lensink (2020), and the aforementioned review of reviews by Duvendack & Mader (2020), from which the theoretical stands outlined in Section 2 were drawn. Added to this can be the excellent pooling exercise of Dahal & Fiala (2020), which combines eight major microcredit RCTs in order to explore the power implications of low take-up rates in these studies.

Whilst these reviews and surveys differ in terms of the number and composition of underlying RCT evidence, methods of discussion and/ or aggregation, and the exact questions asked regarding the bodies of evidence, the conclusions are actually fairly consistent. The conclusions from the main reviews and surveys into microfinance impacts are broadly as follows:

1. The overall positive impacts of microfinance are modest at best, and certainly non-revelatory. Positive effects are fairly small, and not found across all indicators. Some surveys (e.g., Van Rooyen et al. 2012) also document negative side-effects, and negative impacts on certain subgroups.
2. Where there are positive effects, these are stronger for savings products than for microcredit, and are often stronger on consumption indicators and consumption smoothing,[9] rather than on business or investment indicators.

---

[8]   However, it is worth mentioning the set of highly cited and influential RCT studies conducted in eight countries, and discussed and compared by Banerjee et al. (2015b): see Angelucci et al. (2015), Attanasio et al. (2015), Augsburg et al. (2015), Banerjee et al. (2015a), Crépon et al. (2015), and Tarozzi et al. (2015).

[9]   Non-RCT evidence from asking households in developing countries to keep "financial diaries" also suggests a strong consumption-smoothing effect of the availability of microfinance (Collins et al. 2009).

3. As a result of limited impacts on long-term investment, and greater use on household consumption and consumption smoothing, microfinance has had very limited impacts on the profitability and expansion of microenterprises. Additionally, the consumption-smoothing uses tend to alleviate short-term crises rather than stimulating long-term elevation from poverty (Banerjee et al. 2015b). The result is that the long-term impacts of microfinance are more disappointing than the short-run impacts.

4. Many microfinance interventions, especially microcredit, are characterized by low take-up rates. That is, only a small proportion of those to whom credit is made available actually choose to borrow. This suggests either that the latent demand for microcredit is not as great as expected, or that the available products are not being well marketed or explained.[10] Dahal & Fiala (2020) demonstrate that these low take-up rates, and their effects on the *power* of statistical inference to detect significant effects, may be driving the disappointing overall effects of microcredit on economic indicators.

Collectively, these four conclusions may seem quite sobering. There are, however, some reasons for optimism within them. First, if the early emphasis on microcredit was misplaced, and the real latent demand was for savings, a subsequent switch in emphasis may yield more positive results, especially as savings products are less risky to provide. Second, at least there are some positive impacts, so the next generation of microfinance research can focus on how to make these positive impacts larger, rather than having to seek entirely new forms of financial inclusion outreach. This may be happening, for example, in the advent of "Microfinance Plus", which fuses microfinance products with trainings and workshops aimed at helping people make better use of these products (Garcia & Lensink 2019). Focus Box 3.3 discusses the "Poverty Graduation Program", which is an example of financial inclusion interventions combined with a large package of other poverty reduction interventions designed to achieve a sustained "big push" out of absolute poverty for the world's ultra-poor – perhaps the largest and most famous

---

[10] Another possibility is that they differ from what people actually want; for example, many microcredit products come in the form of group lending, and are by definition quite small in terms of amounts. Therefore, if what people actually want is large, individual/anonymous loans, they may not be interested in the offerings of many MFIs whilst open to utilizing other types of credit.

example of a "full package" intervention. Third, if the disappointing results are driven by low take-up rates, this constitutes evidence against the desirability of, and demand for, existing microfinance offerings, rather than evidence against the important of enhanced financial inclusion in general. Improving the desirability of these products, perhaps through a broadening of the focus away from exclusively credit, is therefore a very reasonable avenue of advancement.

What is clear, however, is that microfinance alone is not a panacea for either mass poverty reduction or mass business stimulation in developing countries; the evidence shows that market-generated products and other forms of intervention clearly have a large role to play in boosting financial inclusion, and through it, development outcomes. Hermes & Lensink (2021) note the important empirical regularity that "there is [generally] an inverse relationship between the 'rigour' of the impact study and the size of the impact of microcredit on outcomes. The more a study tries to control for biases, the less positive the results seem to be." This suggests that lack of econometric sophistication is not a viable explanation for the disappointing effects of microfinance interventions, and that the problems lie with the interventions themselves.

Focus box 3.3   Impacts of microfinance: the full package

Microfinance programs are not the only development interventions to have positive but elusively small or transitory impacts on key living standards indicators such as income and poverty. Social provisions, food programs, cash transfers, health interventions, trainings, natal interventions, etc. have all been shown to have positive impacts on poverty reduction in certain settings yet have faced questions over their cost effectiveness and sustainability (Khan & Arefin 2013; Todd 2017). Some researchers have argued that such interventions need to be combined in order to generate a sufficient "big push" out of poverty; implicit in this notion is that there are external scale economies of interventions such that they complement each other and the effects more-than-proportionally interact. The most famous example of such a "full package" approach is the Poverty Graduation Program

(Banerjee et al. 2015b[11]). The Poverty Graduation Program is targeted at the ultra-poor – those in such extreme poverty that even the most basic first steps towards broader social and economic participation are unattainable for them, and has been trialled in numerous developing countries with different social, geographic, and economic contexts. The program involves a one-off large transfer of an asset, temporary cash transfers in the early stages, coaching and training around both business and life skills, and connection to the formal financial system via a savings account and instruction of how to use it. Therefore, the individuals become financially included as just one part of this multi-faceted intervention.

The impacts of the program are noteworthy. Banerjee et al. (2015b) summarizes the results across six different countries, collating the impacts on ten different categories of economic and social outcomes. Causal identification is established via rigorous RCTs of the type discussed elsewhere in this book. It is found that the program has a significantly positive and economically large impact on most of the outcome indicators; specifically on all consumption indicators, all food security indicators, all asset indicators, all positive financial inclusion indicators,[12] all income indicators, and most mental health and political involvement indicators. It performed less well on women empowerment indicators, physical health, and some dimensions of time use.[13] Furthermore, the positive impacts were sustained over one year, and a follow-up study (Banerjee et al. 2021) suggests that many of these

---

[11]   Many specific and individual research papers make up the body of literature around the effects of the Food Graduation Program (FGP); we therefore cite this highly influential overview paper, which is authored by a large set of the researchers involved. The Abdul Latif Jameel Poverty Action Lab (J-PAL) of the Massachusetts Institute of Technology (MIT) website (https://www.povertyactionlab.org/) contains information and links around the full body of FGP research and is a crucial resource for all those interested in policy interventions and rigorous policy evaluations in developing countries.

[12]   The only financial inclusion indicator not impacted is the amount borrowed from informal lenders, something that normatively we would not hope to see increase, although perhaps would have liked to see it decrease. Otherwise, the FGP significantly increased financial inclusion in terms of saving and formal borrowing (credit), the latter of which is not regularly an explicit intervention of the FGP.

[13]   The FGP did increase the total time spent working, but it did not increase the time spent working in either microenterprises or paid employment, which might be considered the most desirable time use outcomes.

positive effects persist for up to 10 years, at least in the Indian context. In terms of impacts, therefore, the program is often considered a great success (USAID 2018).

The evidence from numerous RCTs in different countries and follow-up evaluations is such that these positive findings hold across both time and space. This is, of course, an expensive intervention, and although it is designed to become self-sustaining after initial cost outlays, it has been acknowledged that there is not yet sufficient information as to how it compares with other interventions in terms of cost-effectiveness (Sulaiman et al. 2016). Furthermore, the combined nature of the package makes it difficult to evaluate specifically where the gains are coming from, what are the individual contributions of each component, and whether all are strictly necessary. From our perspective, it is not possible to isolate the importance and contribution of the financial inclusion component. Nevertheless, this is perhaps the most famous example of how interventions – including financial inclusion – can be combined to generate meaningful outcomes, and serves also as a warning about considering the effects of financial inclusion only in isolation.

3.2   General equilibrium effects

A common feature of the RCT evidence on the impacts of microfinance is that they capture the impact of (access to) microfinance interventions on *individual or household outcomes*, as compared with otherwise identical individuals who do not receive (access to) the microfinance intervention. That is, they capture *partial equilibrium effects*. However, as with most exogenous economic shocks, the partial equilibrium impact is by no means the full story. Shocks have feedback effects on other markets and on the local economy, as the direct household changes or effects caused by, for example, access to microcredit, set in motion a chain of additional changes or effects, in response to the original change. This is known as a *multiplier effect*: the initial effect size is multiplied as it goes through this chain. Such effects can also be negative or mitigating, in which case the multiplier is less than one.

Capturing and estimating these multiplier effects is a very difficult task, and beyond the scope of most RCTs. The identifying assumptions of RCTs imply that, whilst differences in outcomes between treatment and control groups can be causally attributed to the interventions, there is no way to causally attribute any other changes out-with the treatment group. Performing RCTs at larger levels of aggregation, for example having control and treatment groups made up of whole provinces, is for the most part prohibitively expensive, and of insufficient sample size to ensure quality randomization. For analysing the general equilibrium effects of microfinance and financial inclusion on the broader local economy, researchers must therefore have recourse to natural experiments. A hugely important recent paper in this regard is Breza & Kinnan (2021), which is sufficiently revelatory to warrant exclusive discussion in this subsection. But see also Focus Box 3.4 for a more theoretical discussion of general equilibrium effects of financial inclusion.

Breza & Kinnan draw attention to the aforementioned potential multiplier effect of microfinance interventions by outlining two channels through which microfinance, especially credit, might have feedback effects on other participants in the local economy who do not directly make use of the credit access. First, it is proposed that microfinance impacts may spillover to the local economy through the channel of increased aggregate demand. As was discussed above, the body of RCT evidence has shown a consistent positive effect of access to microcredit on consumption. As this consumption is mostly spent locally, this will in turn have an impact on local retail businesses and service providers through the additional demand for their products and services, even when these businesses do not have access to, or choose not to avail themselves of, the microcredit. Second, it is proposed that, by improving business outcomes, microfinance may indirectly increase labour demand as businesses expand and hire more, generating higher wages and employment probabilities even for local residents who do not access microfinance themselves. Although the RCT evidence for the business outcome effect is less regular and meaningful than for the consumption effect, Breza & Kinnan argue that, in combination with the aforementioned boost in aggregate demand for the products and services of non-borrowing businesses, which is not captured by the RCTS, the small direct impacts of microfinance on business outcomes that have been detected are likely magnified, which in turn leads to the additional impact of increased labour demand.

In order to test their hypotheses for the effects of microcredit on the local economic outcomes of *non-borrowing* businesses and workers, Breza & Kinnan exploit a natural experiment that makes use of the sudden and unexpected banning of microcredit in one specific state of India, Andhra Pradesh. The authors show that this exogenous shock led to a large negative balance sheet impact to those microfinance firms that were disproportionately present in Andhra Pradesh, without having much impact on microfinance firms that were not present in this state. The affected firms had to dramatically reduce their lending across the rest of India. This implied a *negative exogenous shock* to the availability of microcredit in districts where the major microcredit firms were the same as in Andhra Pradesh, with no concurrent shock to those districts with different lenders. The former therefore form the treatment group (of districts) and the latter the control group in this natural experiment.[14] The authors found that *rural* districts and small towns[15] in which the availability of microcredit was exogenously and sizeably reduced saw large declines in consumption and (average) wages, as compared with those districts that experienced no such reduction.

As the paper has only one source of exogenous variation, it is unable to disentangle the separate contributions of the two proposed channels through which microcredit is proposed to impact economic outcomes out with the direct effect. However, by dividing the point estimate for the total decrease in consumption caused by a one standard deviation decline in the availability of microcredit by the amount of one standard deviation of microcredit, the authors are able to provide a benchmark estimate of the *microcredit multiplier*: 2.9. This means that each dollar (rupee) of withdrawn microcredit led to a 2.9 dollar (rupee) decline in average household consumption. The fact that this multiplier is (much) greater than one demonstrates the indirect/general equilibrium effects – microcredit increases local aggregate consumption by far more than just the

---

[14]   The actual procedure is somewhat more complex than this, with a bounded continuous variable of district level exposure to the microfinance crisis caused by the Andhra Pradesh ban constructed on the basis of the similarity of the local microlender mix to that of Andhra Pradesh, normalized such that the point estimate in a difference-in-differences regression captures the effects of a one-standard deviation increase in exposure to the microfinance crisis on district-level economic outcomes. However, conceptually this can usefully be thought of as a kind of natural RCT where economic outcomes in districts that randomly suffered a reduction in microcredit availability are compared with those in districts that suffered a lesser, or no, such reduction.

[15]   There was no such effect found for districts in cities; it is argued that this is because cities offer far more alternative sources of credit, whereas in rural areas microcredit is often the only (formal sector) option.

spending of the loans. The authors go on to provide suggestive evidence that it is indeed the aggregate demand and labour market channels that are driving this multiplier effect.

The implications of this study are vast, for several reasons: (1) it suggests that the general equilibrium effects of microcredit on local economic outcomes vastly exceed the partial equilibrium effects, and therefore that the RCT evidence *underestimates* the positive impacts of microfinance; (2) it suggests that microfinance, and by extension increased levels of financial inclusion, can have positive impacts *both* on the immediate users of that microfinance (the newly financially included) and on those who do not use it, at the local level; (3) it suggests that microfinance has now become so embedded in local economies that withdrawing the availability of it can do *serious and tangible harm*; and (4) it suggests that the fact the RCT evidence shows microcredit loans are spent more on consumption than on business investment and entrepreneurship may still result in positive long-run outcomes for businesses, because the increased consumption leads to increased demand for the products and services of local businesses. Furthermore, because this indirect positive impact is also felt by non-borrowing businesses, this may explain why some studies failed to find significant differences in business outcomes between control and treatment groups.

There are, of course, some reasonable critiques of the generalizability of this study. As the experimental setting predicates the analysis of the effects of *withdrawing* microcredit from markets in which it is already well established, it may not be the case that adding microcredit to new markets will generate converse positive effects of a similar magnitude. The distribution of negative and positive effects may be asymmetric. Similarly, the shock to microcredit availability was large and unexpected; when households and businesses are better able to plan for the withdrawal (or addition) of credit availability, they may find ways to reduce the consumption impact. Nevertheless, the finding of large, positive, and statistically significant general equilibrium impacts of microcredit on the local economy, and of the potential damage that could be done by ending or reducing microfinance programs, is a strong counter-argument to the recent prevailing trend of the RCT literature in minimizing the impacts of microfinance, especially microcredit, and especially on business outcomes.

Another very interesting recent study that considers impacts of microfinance beyond direct microfinance effects is Agarwal et al. (2021). While Breza & Kinnan consider effects of a *decline* in the supply of microcredit in India, Agarwal et al. (2021) examine the consequences of an *expansion* of the microfinance sector in Rwanda. They show that a government-subsidized microcredit expansion in Rwanda not only increased access to microcredit for unbanked individuals but also raised access to credit from commercial banks. The mechanism was as follows. When individuals took up a loan from the (newly established) microfinance organisation, their information including all lending activities is submitted to a credit bureau, which could be used by other lenders. Unbanked individuals therefore were able to build up a credit history with the microfinance sector, which enabled them to obtain access to relatively cheap credit from commercial banks. The microfinance sector thus helped to reduce the costly asymmetric information between poor borrowers and commercial banks. Most importantly, the microfinance rollout program, partly due to the positive spillover effect, resulted in reduced poverty rates in less developed areas. This again confirms that impacts of microfinance may be much bigger than suggested by studies that relied on partial equilibrium effects only, such as most recent RCTs.

Focus box 3.4 Financial inclusion, entrepreneurship, and total factor productivity growth

A series of papers examine possible benefits of financial inclusion using general equilibrium models with financial frictions. Many of these papers use adjusted versions of the occupational choice model, which has become a workhorse model for the macro-development literature (see e.g., Banerjee & Newman 1993; Lloyd-Ellis & Bernhardt 2000; Besley et al. 2021; and Dabla-Norris et al. 2021). The occupational choice model typically considers a world with heterogeneous agents i, who differ in terms of the amount of own wealth b_i and fixed start-up costs (which are inversely related to entrepreneurial talent) to begin a business, x_i.

Agents maximize utility by choosing to become a worker or an entrepreneur. Those agents who choose to be a worker, supply one unit of labour inelastically, and receive an equilibrium wage w in return. Agents who choose to become an entrepreneur, use capital k and labour l as inputs to produce output, and earn profits, which depend on the agent's productivity, labour, and capital costs.

Jeong and Townsend (2007) use the occupational choice model to explain the impact of financial inclusion. They assume that there are two groups of agents. The first group, the so-called credit group, has access to financial markets, and can borrow and lend freely at the equilibrium interest rate r of the credit market. The second group, named the non-credit group, does not have access to financial markets at all, and thus has to self-finance both the start-up costs as well as the (working) capital costs. The fraction of the population with access to credit is exogenously given by a *financial inclusion* parameter p. An increase in p indicates an increase in financial inclusion. The financial inclusion parameter may reflect high transaction costs that agents may face, for instance due to their geographical location – that is, the distance to a bank branch.

Agents in the 'non-credit' sector face a borrowing constraint, which is modelled as: $0 \leq k_i \leq b_i - x_i$. The borrowing constraint implies that the maximum amount of (working) capital that can be used is positively related to own wealth and negatively to the fixed start-up costs (or positively to entrepreneurial talent, depending on the interpretation of x). The borrowing constraint may imply that even very talented agents cannot become entrepreneurs if their own wealth is too low to finance any capital, which is clearly an inefficient outcome as in principle all talented agents should be able to become entrepreneurs. For entrepreneurs in the 'credit' sector, the borrowing constraint does not exist and everybody will borrow in line with efficiency rules.

Given initial wealth and the equilibrium market wage, it is possible to determine a marginal level of start-up costs (or talent) z^m for which the agent is indifferent between becoming an entrepreneur or a wageworker for both sectors. An important feature of the model is that the marginal level of start-up costs for agents in the non-credit and credit sector differs. Let's first consider the marginal level of start-up costs for agents in the non-credit sector. Define x^m as the level of start-up costs for which profits π are equal to the wage rate w: x^m is implicitly given by the following condition: $\pi\left(b_i, x^m, w\right) = w$. If an agent's start-up costs are above x^m, she will become a wageworker for sure as entrepreneurial profits will be below the wage obtained as a wageworker. However, by considering the budget constraint, it is immediately clear that start-up costs cannot exceed own wealth to begin with, as capital cannot be negative. This implies that the marginal level of start-up costs below which an agent decides to become an entrepreneur is given by:

$$z(b_i, w) = min\left[b_i, x^m(b_i, w) \right]$$

The marginal level of talent for agents in the non-credit sector thus depends on own wealth b and the market wage rate w. For the non-credit sector, the occupational choice can be partitioned into four areas, see Figure 3.3 below: (1) agents for which start-up costs are so high (or entrepreneurial talent so low), say z^*, that regardless of their own wealth, they will always become a wage worker (the area of unconstrained wage workers); (2) agents for whom start-up costs are below z^*, but own wealth is too low to finance fixed start-up costs (the area of constrained wage workers); (3) agents with sufficient own wealth to run profitable business, but their scale of business is constrained – that is, fixed start-up costs can be financed, but wealth is not enough to fund unconstrained level of (working) capital; and (4) agents with sufficient amount of own wealth to finance fixed start-up costs and unconstrained level of working capital: the unconstrained entrepreneurs.

Figure 3.3 provides an example of the occupational choice for the non-credit sector

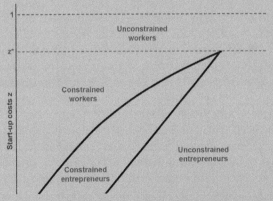

Figure 3.3   Model of occupational choice without credit access (imperfect financial inclusion)

For agents in the credit-group, the optimization process differs. As they are not credit constrained, the occupational choice is not affected by own wealth, but only by their entrepreneurial talent. Figure 3.4 explains the occupational choice:

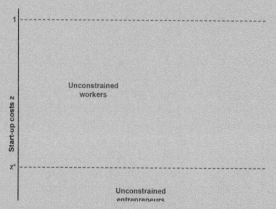

Figure 3.4   Model of occupational choice with credit access (perfect financial inclusion)

Note that the percentages of different types of agents, for each level of wealth, are relatively simple to determine as start-up costs are uniformly distributed between 0 and 1. This implies that, for agents in the credit sector, the percentage of (unconstrained) entrepreneurs is independent of the level of wealth, and always equals z^*, whereas the percentage of (unconstrained) workers is always equal to $1-z^*$. For agents in the non-credit sector, the analysis is a bit more complicated as percentages of entrepreneurs now also depend on the wealth level. For poor agents, indicated by b_{low}, the percentages of unconstrained entrepreneurs is 0; the percentages of unconstrained workers is $1-z^*$, the percentage of constrained workers equals $z^*-0.1$ and the percentage of constrained entrepreneurs equals 0.1. For rich entrepreneurs, indicated by b_{high} the percentage of unconstrained entrepreneurs is z^* and the percentage of unconstrained workers is $1-z^*$. For this level of wealth, there are no constrained workers and entrepreneurs. Most importantly, whilst the percentage of (unconstrained) entrepreneurs is independent of wealth for credit-sector agents, it increases in wealth for non-credit sector agents. This implies that, for poor agents, the percentage of unconstrained entrepreneurs is smaller in the non-credit sector than in the credits sector, whilst the opposite is true for rich agents.

It is now relatively easy to see what the impact of financial inclusion on entrepreneurship will be. Financial inclusion implies that the weight of the credit-sector increases vis-à-vis the non-credit sector in the aggregate economy. If we ignore for simplicity secondary equilibrium effects via changes in factor prices (equilibrium wages and interest rates), financial inclusion will increase entrepreneurship for poor agents, but will decrease entrepreneurship amongst rich agents. A main reason is that, for agents in the credit sector who have low entrepreneurial talents, the incentive to become entrepreneurs is low. Instead of becoming an entrepreneur, they will choose to be a wageworker and deposit their wealth in banks that may earn high interest income in addition to the wage income. Thus, the impact of financial inclusion on entrepreneurship is ambiguous: financial inclusion will probably increase entrepreneurship for poor economies, whilst it will decrease entrepreneurship for wealthy economies.

Jeong and Townsend (2007) calibrate the full model on data for Thailand to examine the main sources of total factor productivity (TFP) growth, which is commonly assumed to be exogenous. Their simulations suggest that financial inclusion is the dominant factor driving TFP growth: about 70% of Thai TFP growth can be explained from financial deepening! This study thus clearly shows the importance of financial inclusion for aggregate TFP and hence aggregate GDP growth.

4.   Impacts of government and banking interventions

The paper by Agarwal et al. (2021) is related to an influential earlier literature on the impact of expansions of commercial bank programs on financial inclusion and welfare. Whilst microfinance remains the primary tool of policy interventions aimed at boosting levels of financial inclusion, a large amount of financial products and services are still provided by conventional banks. In some cases, banks find it optimal from a business perspective to adopt expansion strategies aimed at attracting the unbanked and therefore boosting financial inclusion, such as Equity Bank in Kenya as discussed in Focus Box 1.2. In most cases, however, the social benefits from opening new branches in previously underserved areas may far outweigh the private benefits to the banks themselves – this is why there are no or limited banking services in these areas to begin with. In these cases, banks only open branches in such areas when encouraged or required to do so by policymakers and government, either via subsidies or coercive legislation. Sometimes, governments also use conventional banks and bank branch expansions as channels to link other financial inclusion outreach programs, such as the Self-Help Groups in India analysed by Swamy (2014). In instances such as these, governments exploit their monopoly power in the allocation of banking licences or approvals for new branch expansions; for example, the government can refuse to permit branch expansions unless a certain number of the new branches are located in underserved areas, or unless the new branches are linked with other FI interventions such as the self-help groups.

Opportunities to evaluate the impact of increases in financial inclusion through conventional banks are more limited than through microfinance interventions. Whilst microfinance interventions are often performed in partnership with international policymakers and researchers and therefore have measurement and evaluation strategies built into the rollout, commercial bank expansions must usually be analysed *ex post*, and private banks may be very resistant to providing data. Causal identification of the effects of financial inclusion requires at least quasi-random allocation of the location of new bank branches or access to banking services, but commercial banks choose their locations and target customers for strategic and deliberately non-random reasons. Nevertheless, there are some occasions where natural experiments present themselves when bank branches become "as good as randomly assigned", either as a result of government interventions of the type discussed above or due to other context-specific circumstances. These relatively rare occasions can provide powerful insights into the impacts of financial inclusion when exploited by researchers in a sophisticated manner, not least because the volume and magnitude of financial products and services offered by commercial banks can be much larger than those provided by microfinance institutions. This section will discuss the results of two such sophisticated studies; an investigation into the impacts of a government-led social banking experiment in India (Burgess & Pande 2005), and an analysis of the impacts of a massive and quasi-random bank branch expansion by Banco Azteca in Mexico (Bruhn & Love 2014). Both of these papers yield optimistic conclusions about the impacts of financial inclusion alleviating poverty.

Burgess & Pande (2005) focus on a specific large-scale component of a long-term government strategy to improve financial access for the rural poor in India. This component was a 1977 (until 1990) policy of the Indian Central Bank to only grant permission for banks to open a new branch in a currently banked area if they also opened four new branches in unbanked areas, known as the 1:4 rule. This implied that banks wishing to benefit from the additional profits associated with increasing service to large markets were required also to increase service into areas that they did not otherwise consider profitable. The financial inclusion impact that Burgess & Pande seek to isolate is the *causal effect* of an additional rural (previously unbanked) bank branch on the poverty headcount ratio of the Indian state in which the new bank branch is located. In other words: does increasing the number of people who can access financial services in a state reduce the level of severe poverty in that state? By using the introduction of the 1:4 rule in 1977 and the removal of it in 1991 as exogenous breaks in the time-trend of the opening of rural branches, the authors are able to causally estimate the poverty impact of additional rural branches. They do this by instrumenting the annual state number of rural bank branches per capita with a linear trend break model based on exploiting the break in the relationship between the *initial* number of rural bank branches per capita and rural expansion in the different policy periods.[16] The authors find that each additional rural bank branch causally reduced the state-wide level of absolute poverty, with a point estimate of a 4.74% reduction in the state-wide poverty headcount ratio per each additional rural branch. This established a causal impact of increased financial inclusion, through providing conventional banking services in previously unbanked locations, on poverty reduction.

Whilst Burgess & Pande (2005) exploit exogenous variation in the placement of rural bank branches brought about by government intervention,

---

[16]   Specifically, at the times when the 1:4 rule was not in place (before 1977 and after 1990), a higher initial level of rural branches per capita was positively associated with new branch expansion because these were states where rural branches were more profitable. In the period when the 1:4 rule was in place, 1977–1990, a higher initial level of bank branches per capita was negatively associated with new branch expansion because banks were coerced by the government into opening branches in more unbanked areas. By separately incorporating both of these effects into the instrument, the authors isolate only that component of new rural branch expansion which was as a direct result of the exogenous timing of the 1:4 policy.

Bruhn & Love (2014) utilize the unique branch expansion strategy of Banco Azteca in Mexico in 2002 in order to establish quasi-random allocation of new branches. The key to this strategy was that Banco Azteca opened a huge number of new branches, >800, at exactly the same time, *within* existing locations of a consumer goods store called Grupo Elektra. That is, the location of the new bank branches was predetermined by the locations of Grupo Elektra stores, rather than chosen on the basis of the perceived profitability of the local financial services market. The identification strategy, difference-in-differences, then relies on comparing the *before-and-after* trends in new business openings, income levels, and employment probabilities in the municipalities with a new Banco Azteca branch with those in municipalities which do not receive a new branch. In essence, the allocation of a Banco Azteca branch is an *experimental treatment*, and the municipalities that receive a branch are the treatment group, whilst the control group are those municipalities which do not receive a branch. The locating of branches in pre-existing stores ensures quasi-random allocation of the treatment, and the comparison of before-and-after trends implies that other time-invariant differences between the treatment and control municipalities are parcelled out of the treatment effect. The result of this analysis is that the average municipality that received a Banco Azteca branch experienced a larger number of informal businesses, higher average income levels, and lower unemployment rates, as compared to those municipalities which did not receive a branch. This then suggests that the new bank branches, and the increased financial inclusion they brought about, created new (informal) businesses and jobs, and raised incomes. The authors interpret this as an overall impact of financial inclusion on poverty reduction.

It is noted by the author that Banco Azteca is comparable to microfinance providers (MFIs) in the size and scale of its financial products – that is, offering small loans to low- and middle-income groups. Banco Azteca therefore caters to a different customer base from most other commercial banks. This implies that the results observed are due at least in part to increased financial inclusion, rather than additional banking alternatives offered to individuals who are already financially included. However, it may also imply that the results would not generalize to bank branch expansions of larger conventional banks, and may be more in line with what one would expect from MFI branch expansions. Despite this, there are some key differences between Banco Azteca and most MFIs: Banco Azteca is funded by its own deposits rather than international donor money and is at least designed as a self-sustaining profit-making bank; Banco Azteca is not branded as an MFI and does not carry the same connotations; and the synergy between Banco Azteca and the Grupo Elektra stores owned by a parent company allow for much larger economies of scale and information and collection mechanisms than most MFIs have access to. It is not therefore appropriate to expect this result to generalize to microfinance providers, although the structure and advantages of Banco Azteca may provide some guidance as to how certain MFIs can operate more successfully.

The message of this section is that, when we are able to accurately measure it, the causal impact of increased financial inclusion through branch expansions of conventional banks is one of poverty reduction and positive microenterprise and income effects. The identification techniques of the above-discussed papers have allowed us to confirm that these impacts are present when banks expand into previously unserved markets – true increases occur in financial inclusion – at least within these specific contexts. The normative question of *how* to achieve such expansions remains. Whilst such expansions have been shown to improve economic outcomes for unbanked residents, there is in many cases a business reason why conventional banks are not currently serving these residents. One option is to use government coercion to force or incentivize such branch expansions, such as in the Indian example. Another is to emphasize to banks that different business models, such as those pioneered by Equity Bank and Banco Azteca, can turn serving the unbanked into a profitable strategy. The former option, however, introduces other distortions into the market and comes at the cost of harming bank profits and reducing the levels of banking services overall; the latter requires willingness and flexibility on behalf of banking sectors, which may have become somewhat entrenched in traditional banking models. A third option is to introduce additional, government-backed players into the financial services market with a specific financial inclusion and outreach focus – which brings us back to microfinance.

5.   Impacts at the macro level

Whilst the empirical research into the impacts of financial inclusion is extensive and rich, there is as yet relatively little rigorous econometric analysis of the causal effects of financial inclusion on country-level macroeconomic development indicators such as growth, aggregate investment, total factor productivity, and inequality. The study of Breza & Kinnan (2021) discussed extensively in Section 3.2 does capture positive effects of microcredit on wages and consumption at the regional level, and does so in a manner that includes the average impacts on the entire local populations, rather than just those who are recipients of microcredit. Nevertheless, it is still difficult to envision the extent to which these results 'aggregate upwards' to national-level relationships, and the indicators investigated are still household level wages and consumption rather than broader aggregates.

To investigate macro-level impacts, a research question would need to take a form such as, "What is the average causal effect of an increase in [for example] the proportion of the population with a bank account on GDP growth [or income inequality, or total factor productivity] in developing country economies?" Simple correlations, however, would be insufficient to capture this causal effect – it would be impossible to unpick the effects of financial inclusion (indicators) on growth from the effects of growth on financial inclusion. Such questions, therefore, are rife with potential endogeneity biases, and more sophisticated econometric analysis is necessary. Omar & Inaba (2020) approach this issue by using panel fixed effects regressions, which remove some components of endogeneity bias, specifically those driven by country-specific time-invariant heterogeneity. They regress poverty headcount measures and GINI coefficients[17] on an index of financial inclusion, for a panel of 116 developing countries, and find that in both cases the coefficient on the FI index is significantly negative – that is, increases in financial inclusion lead to decreases in poverty and income inequality in the average sample country. There is, however, some doubt as to whether a simple panel FE identification strategy is sufficient to alleviate all forms of endogeneity bias; for example, if both the increases in FI and decreases in poverty are driven by some third variable, such as international aid, and this variable varies both over time and between countries, the panel FE approach would fail to account for this bias.

---

[17]   The GINI coefficient is a commonly used single-variable indicator of income inequality that is bounded between zero and one and increases as the income distribution in a country becomes more unequal.

Other papers that seek to establish the link between financial inclusion and inequality and/or growth at the national level include Banerjee et al. (2020), and Chima et al. (2021). The former utilizes the general method of moments (GMM) technique to investigate the effects of an index of financial inclusion on growth and income equality, as well as some human capital and health outcomes. They find a significantly positive effect of FI on growth and a significantly negative effect on income inequality,[18] the latter finding being consistent with that of Omar & Inaba (2020). Banerjee et al. (2020) add to the set of papers that provide at least suggestive evidence of positive macro-level effects of financial inclusion, and add to the literature by additionally decomposing their FI index into measures of *access*, *usage*, and *quality*, and showing that most of their results are driven only by actual usage rather than merely access. This relates to the discussion in Chapter 1 about the need to take care with different FI measures, and of the important of designing and providing FI products and services that people actually use. Chima et al. (2021) use system-GMM as well and also conclude that FI has a positive effect on growth rates, this time specifically within Sub-Saharan Africa.

From the above discussion, it can be seen that the small body of literature thus far suggests a positive impact of financial inclusion on growth and income equality at the national level, at least when the FI measures capture usage of, rather than merely access to, financial products and services. However, much more research is needed in this area, and more rigorous causal identification techniques will be required for this question to be anywhere close to settled. The positive associations, and positive effects through system-GMM estimates, are encouraging, as are the positive general equilibrium effects rigorously uncovered by Breza & Kinnan (2021). We can hope that a future wave of research will uncover other opportunities to exploit natural experiments and exogenous sources of variation at the national level in order to pin down these macroeconomic effects of financial inclusion in a more comprehensive and rigorous manner.

---

[18]   Again, as measured by the GINI coefficient, such that a negative effect implies a reduction in inequality.

6.   Conclusion

The story of this review of the research regarding the impacts of financial inclusion is one of tempered optimism. On the one hand, many rigorously conducted impact studies, such as RCTs, have suggested that (access to) microfinance – especially in the form of microcredit – only has a relatively small impact on people's lives. On the other hand, however, more recent studies that try to go beyond the partial equilibrium effects, seem much more positive about the impact of financial inclusion interventions in general and microfinance interventions in particular. Most importantly, there is a growing evidence that increases in the number of people who have access to, and make use of, financial products and services translate into meaningful economic and social impacts, be they poverty reduction, increases in income, positive business outcomes, or consumption smoothing. However, this positive note does not automatically imply that financial inclusion has similar effects for everybody. It may, for instance, be the case that impacts of financial inclusion are different for men as compared with women, an issue we will discuss in detail in the next two chapters.

4. Women and financial inclusion, Part I: gains and disparities

1. Introduction: women, finance, and development

In 2016, the government of the Democratic Republic of Congo amended Law 16-008, commonly known as the 'Family Code'. This amendment allowed, for the first time, married women to open bank accounts, register businesses, and apply for credit without the signed approval of their husband or guardian. A World Bank (2019) study into international gender differences in property and inheritance law reported that 75 of 187 economies surveyed still had laws in place restricting women's rights to manage assets – even when these laws do not directly restrict female financial access such as in the DRC, they indirectly restrict it by systematically reducing the financial property rights and holdings of assets, and therefore of collateral, by women as compared with men. The recent, and in some cases current, existence of such formalized discrimination against women in terms of their financial access and self-determination is just one of the reasons we continue to observe wide gender gaps in financial inclusion, and why the gender dimension is so crucial both to the study of financial inclusion and to the formulation of policy.

A key feature of the financial inclusion concept, as compared with that of financial development, is that from the title itself there is a focus on equality and inclusivity. Therefore, equality of financial access between genders, as between other groups, is by definition a key element of financial inclusion. As has been noted in previous chapters, financial *exclusion* can take place across a number of dimensions; individuals can be financially excluded voluntarily or for non-systematic reasons, and groups can be subject to *systematic involuntary exclusion* from the financial system on the basis of ethnicity, tribe, age, social class, religion, legal status, geographic location, and of course gender. However, in most cases, the systematic financial exclusion of such groups is somewhat context specific. Reducing financial discrimination on the basis of tribe in Nigeria, race in Brazil, social caste in India, residency in the south of Vietnam, or migrant-worker status in Qatar is crucially important to improving financial inclusion within those countries, but generalizes little beyond them. However, this is not the case with financial discrimination on the basis of gender. Whilst some of the reasons for gendered financial exclusion may be context specific, and whilst the gender gap in financial inclusion does vary in magnitude between countries and geographic regions, the overall existence of this gender gap appears to be a worldwide stylized fact. The financial exclusion of women is a global phenomenon.

The paragraph above already indicates much of the explanation for why the financial inclusion of women is such an important and specific priority for development researchers and policymakers, and why the topic warrants specific chapters in this book. There is, however, even more to it than that. There is evidence to suggest that, not only is the enhanced financial inclusion of women desirable in terms of equality and of closing the gender gap, but that improving the financial access of women can actually yield *more* positive societal benefits than improving that of men (Duflo 2012). Additionally, enhanced financial inclusion of women can yield positive impacts beyond merely economic effects; financial inclusion is seen by many as a tool by which greater women empowerment and preservation of the rights of women can be achieved (Pitt et al. 2006; Chliova et al. 2015; see also Armendáriz & Morduch, 2010, Chapter 5). On this basis, we propose the following set of five layered reasons why a specific focus on the financial inclusion of women is of paramount importance:

1. the fact that there exists a gap in the level of financial access between men and women is alone *sufficient reason* for why this gap should be closed;
2. the fact that this gap is a global phenomenon, observable in every developing region of the world, renders the financial inclusion of women a *global priority*;

3. closing this gender gap represents one of the most efficient ways of increasing *overall levels of financial inclusion*, because many unbanked women clearly represent 'low hanging fruit', in that, if the men in their community are already financially included, the financial products and services must be available there and supply is therefore not the binding constraint;

4. in addition to the closure of the gender gap yielding increases in the overall level of financial inclusion, there is evidence to suggest that newly financially included women may actually use these financial services *better* than men in their communities, in terms of generating positive economic outcomes;

5. finally, the gains in equality generated by closing the gender gap may have knock-on empowerment effects for women and communities beyond traditional economic and development measures.

Note that these reasons build upon each other, such that, even if the latter reasons do not hold in certain countries or contexts, this in no way invalidates those that come before. Each of the above reasons individually represents fairly compelling arguments for the critical importance of the gender aspect of financial inclusion, but when they are taken together, the argument becomes overwhelming. Much of this chapter and the next will elaborate and support each of the above reasons, providing evidence both for the current existence, prevalence, and persistence of the gender gap in financial inclusion in the developing world, and for the potential gains that may be realized by its closure. There are, however, cases when providing support in terms of finance and financial access to women have not yielded the expected positive economic results. For example, De Mel et al. (2008) using a field experiment in Sri Lanka find that cash grants to female entrepreneurs do not increase profits, whilst cash grants to male entrepreneurs significantly enhance profits. Moreover, there is also evidence, in particular from the microfinance literature, that certain forms of access to finance sometimes even have a negative impact on women empowerment women empowerment in some specific contexts when other latent issues remain unaddressed (for a discussion, see e.g. Hansen et al. 2021). It is important also to note and understand these 'failures' so that policy can be tailored accordingly. Whilst it is tempting to become excited about the potential gains from improving the financial inclusion of women, especially along the dimension of women empowerment and emancipation, it is necessary to also remain circumspect; there is no single 'magic bullet' for empowering the women of the world, and financial inclusion will always remain just one small part of the package of policies and changes necessary for achieving this aim, which is so critical both for development and for society.

The rest of this chapter is organized as follows. Section 2 will elaborate on why it is important to focus on women and section 3 presents empirical evidence on the financial inclusion gender gap. Section 4 concludes.

2.   The importance of focusing on women

A recent systematic review of reviews (Duvendack & Mader 2020) synthesized the findings of the vast literature on financial inclusion programs in a highly rigorous manner. Meta-analyses, which had already sought to combine the results from multiple studies into specific financial inclusion interventions, were evaluated on the basis of an objective quality criteria, with the 'best eleven' then being treated as a combined body of evidence and analysed in terms of what they collectively told us about the findings of the impacts of such interventions. We will have more to say about these findings later, but for now we draw attention to this striking fact: "all 11 meta-studies took an interest in gender and women's empowerment in one way or another" (Duvendack & Mader 2020, p. 608). This serves to illustrate how central the gender dimension has become to the study of financial inclusion. This review of reviews in no way sought out exclusively meta-analyses that concerned themselves with gender, and yet no quality meta-analysis that was found neglected to incorporate the gender aspect. Why has the focus on women become so central and ubiquitous across the financial inclusion literature?

A good place to begin answering this question is a seminal paper of Duflo (2012). In this article, Duflo extensively laid out the symbiotic, bi-directional relationship between women empowerment and economic development. The necessity of a dual focus on these two development aims is a clear conclusion of this article; as a result of the recurring finding that a focus purely on general development is insufficient to guarantee advances in women empowerment, it is argued, "continuous policy commitment to equality for its own sake may be needed to bring about equality between men and women." The relevance of this conclusion to the specific field of financial inclusion is clear: growth of overall levels of financial inclusion in many developing regions has *not* predicated closures over time in the gender gaps. It seems, therefore, that these gender gaps will not close fully unless there is a specific focus on doing so.

An important corollary of the above conclusion of Duflo is that the direction of causality between women empowerment and economic development runs both ways. This means that, not only is a specific policy focus on gender desirable because it is necessary for the attainment of closer gender equality, it is desirable also because this closer gender equality itself serves to bring about more economic development. In the financial inclusion context, this is because there are believed to be *specific advantages* to providing financial access and services to women, beyond merely the advantage of improving gender equality by doing so. Duflo notes, "micro-credit schemes, for example, have been directed almost exclusively at women, because, it is argued, women invest the money in goods and services that improve the well-being of families, in goods that are conducive to development." This points to the belief that, in some contexts, women in developing countries *use resources differently* than men (Benhassine et al. 2015). And whilst Duflo is careful to point out that just because women spend differently does not necessarily mean they spend better, she notes a litany of examples of policy interventions where enhanced women empowerment led to overall efficiency-enhancing outcomes for the community as a whole (Udry 1996; Goldstein & Udry 2008).

The reasons, therefore, for focusing on women are both ethical and practical. This is clearly noted by Hansen et al. (2021), who point out that microfinance institutions (MFIs) often target women for the business reason that their repayment rates are believed to be higher than men, and also for the ethical reason that it is believed they will invest in safer and less risky projects (Armendáriz & Morduch 2010; D'Espallier et al. 2011). It is stated that, on average, 80% of MFI creditors are women. Hansen et al. repeat also the point that there may be spending differences between men and women in developing countries, stating that women "are biased to within-household expenditures, such as children's health and education" (Hansen et al. 2021, p. 165). There is now considerable evidence that household expenditure patterns differ depending on which household member generates income, even if total household income remains the same (Duflo and Udry 2004). Focus Box 4.1 explores in greater depth the question as to whether women in developing countries spend differently to men. An even more important point, however, is that these differences in spending preferences need not only manifest when women themselves have more resources to spend. If, as a result of increased women empowerment, women are able to exercise greater influence over *household resources*, overall household spending patterns may shift in the direction of the women's preferences. This distinction is very important. For example, if all that mattered was the gender of the person *spending* the money, in a scenario in which women had access to financial services that men did not, but handed over the money to their husbands to spend, the fact that it was the wife who had *access* to the service and not the husband would be of little relevance. If, however, the woman's having exclusive access to the service increases her bargaining power within the household, and the influence she therefore wields over household decision making, then the spending patterns of the household could be observed to change *even if* it is the husband who still does all the actual spending. This again serves to illustrate the key symbiosis between women empowerment and economic development, with gender-focused financial inclusion fitting in as a potential, if conditional, driver of both.

Focus box 4.1   Do women in developing countries spend differently?

Most financial inclusion development policy and projects explicitly target women, in part because it is believed that they will make socially optimal use of the products and services offered as compared with men. This assumption is specific to developing country contexts and does not imply any innate difference between men and women, merely an understanding of the need to be mindful of societal contexts and constructs. In many such societal contexts, women have more direct responsibilities over children, and therefore consider child welfare as a higher priority when allocating scarce resources (World Bank 2011). Furthermore, most single-parent households in developing countries are headed by women (Chamie 2016), implying that, if gains in financial inclusion and other development policies are concentrated amongst men, the children of these families may be neglected. There is also an evidence-backed belief that women in developing countries use financial products and services more responsibly, leading to higher repayment rates and less risk taking in making use of funds (Armendáriz & Morduch 2010; D'Espallier et al. 2011; Hansen et al. 2021). This makes women more attractive customers of financial inclusion programs from a business perspective, although it should be noted that, in entrepreneurship, lack of risk taking is not always a good thing. Moreover, as has been shown by De Mel et al. (2009), men are more likely to turn a cash grant into profitable investments than women, as women often don't invest the cash grant in their enterprise, and thus are less likely to contribute to an increase in income. This highlights the need to be mindful of the fact that, whilst in general the different spending preferences of women are optimal from the perspective of societal welfare, they may not be optimal in the context of every financial inclusion product or service (De Mel et al. 2009; Duflo 2012).

The empirical evidence around the differential spending preferences of men and women in developing country contexts is larger than can be fully reviewed here. Beaman et al. (2012) found that increasing political representation of women at the local level in India changed political decision-making, with increases in the provision of public goods such as clean water and sanitation, and increases in the local levels of educational attainment for girls. Duflo (2003) found that an exogenous unexpected increase in household resources in the form of a new state pension in South Africa led to nutrition gains in children living with female pension recipients, but not in those living with male pension recipients. More directly related to financial inclusion, a recent paper by Suri & Jack (2016) showed that increases in access to mobile money services in Kenya increased household consumption overall, and that this increase was much larger in female-headed households. They concluded, with evidence, that this greater positive impact of financial inclusion on women than on men came from the effect of financial inclusion (a) on female occupational choice, by allowing them to rely less on multiple-income streams and instead to specialize, and (b) on the ability of women to exercise more direct control over household resources and remittances. This second conclusion in particular implies that the result may in part be driven by differential use of resources.

There are, however, reasons to be mindful of the unintended consequences of financial inclusion programs that are female focused as a result of the expectation that women will use the products and services differently. Koczberski (1998) warns us against the dangerous assumption that women are under-utilized in developing countries and therefore have the capacity to easily take on more work; whilst it is true that there is a large gender gap in labour force participation rates, a lot of women work very hard in the household or in the informal sector, and therefore may not welcome investment or entrepreneurship responsibilities if these are piled on top of what they already have to do. In an ideal world, these investment or entrepreneurship opportunities would allow women to spend less time on household work, or for household work to be divided more equally between the family members; however in practice such a result is unlikely to be achieved without concomitant shifts in attitudes about what constitutes 'a woman's role'.

Additionally, Duflo (2012) notes that the fact that women bear the brunt of household crises or shortages might imply that they are by necessity more short-termist in their spending preferences; the aforementioned Beaman et al. (2012) study did point out that the increases in public good provision resulting from increased female political participation did often prioritize public goods of immediate utility, such as clean water and sanitation, over public goods that yielded delayed utility, such as education facilities. This ties in with the findings of De Mel et al. (2009), who, contrary to their initial expectations, found that female microenterprise owners were not able to generate increased business profits from receiving a large one-off business grant, whereas male microenterprise owners were. The authors had expected to see the opposite results, under the assumption that the women were more credit constrained than men, and therefore would have been able to generate greater marginal gains with the additional funds. The conclusions of the authors, for which they provided extensive evidence, was that they had overlooked the impact of social pressures on the ability of female business owners to be profitable. To give just two examples: (a) because the range of businesses in which it was socially acceptable for women to operate was constrained, women were often operating in saturated markets or in businesses that were not optimal for the deployment of additional resources, therefore reducing greatly their incentive to make additional investments; and (b) because women face additional household pressures, they could not always utilize additional resources optimally, often having to invest the resources in durable investments rather than keeping it on hand as working capital, for fear of having the cash taken from them by their husbands. Whenever investment decisions are made for reasons other than their profit-maximization potential, profitability will necessarily suffer. This important paper therefore demonstrates; (a) the danger of operating purely on assumptions about the gender-differentiated results of financial outreach programs; and (b) the critical importance of incorporating knowledge over context-specific behavioural biases and gender-based social constraints when developing gender-focused financial inclusion programs and policies.

3.   The financial inclusion gender gap

3.1   The gender gap: reasons and evidence

Whilst gender inequalities in financial access and financial inclusion have been known about for some time, the World Bank Global Findex Database, beginning in 2011, has allowed us to empirically verify the existence of the problem and to gain an impression of its scale. Table 4.1 replicates Table 1.3 from Chapter 1, with the addition of the global differentials, and the total differentials by country income group.

From Table 4.1 we can immediately observe, (a) the worldwide ubiquity of the gender gap in financial inclusion,[1] and (b) its relative stubbornness, at least within this short sample-period. Even in some of the regions where the gender gap has closed between 2011 and 2017, such as East Asia & Pacific (EAP), there can be observed a reversal in the trend between 2014 and 2017. In other regions, such as Sub-Saharan Africa (SSA), the gender gap has considerably widened over time. Whilst SSA no longer stands out as the worst overall performer in terms of gendered financial inclusion, it does stand out by having the worst relative decline over the sample period, with the gender gap more than doubling in terms of access to accounts.

Recall that these widening gaps do not necessary mean that increasing numbers of women are being *excluded* from financial access. In most cases, the gaps will be widening because additional men are becoming financially included at a faster rate than additional women. But what this does imply is that, insofar as there have been improvements in financial inclusion across all developing regions, this improvement has often *not been inclusive*, as the widening gender gaps denote improvements in financial inclusion that are highly biased towards men.

The inclusion in the table of the average gender gaps by country income categories also creates an interesting pattern. When looking at the gap

---

[1]   However, there are some individual countries where the gender gap is positive in at least the latest 2017 round: Argentina, Bulgaria, Belarus, Georgia, Indonesia, Kazakhstan, Lesotho, Moldova, Mongolia, Namibia, the Philippines, Russia, South Africa, and some high-income countries. Many of these countries are former members of the Soviet Union, which had an explicit, although not always effective, focus on gender equality throughout its existence (Usha 2005).

Table 4.1   Evolution of gender differential between aggregate financial inclusion indicators by developing region since 2011

Gender Differential (Women–Men)

Share of 15+ individuals with a formal bank account

	2011	2014	2017
World	-8.1%	-7.1%	-7.4%
East Asia & Pacific	-5.7%	-4.0%	-5.3%
Europe & Central Asia	-9.9%	-2.7%	-6.1%
Latin America & Caribbean	-9.3%	-5.7%	-6.5%
Middle East and North Africa	-14.6%	N/A	-17.4%
South Asia	-15.9%	-17.7%	-10.9%
Sub-Saharan Africa	-5.0%	-8.6%	-11.5%
Low Income	-4.8%	-6.7%	-10.1%
Lower Middle Income	-10.8%	-12.4%	-9.7%
Upper Middle Income	-9.3%	-5.8%	-7.7%
High Income	-4.3%	-0.8%	-1.6%

Share of 15+ individuals who received a formal loan in the previous 12 months

	2011	2014	2017
World	-1.9%	-2.3%	-2.8%
East Asia & Pacific	-1.6%	-1.6%	-2.6%
Europe & Central Asia	-1.0%	-1.1%	-2.7%
Latin America & Caribbean	-0.9%	-2.8%	-2.1%
Middle East and North Africa	-2.1%	N/A	-2.0%
South Asia	-1.6%	-2.6%	-2.8%
Sub-Saharan Africa	-1.0%	-1.1%	-1.9%
Low Income	-0.6%	-1.2%	-1.3%
Lower Middle income	-1.1%	-1.9%	-2.2%

Gender Differential (Women–Men)			
Upper Middle Income	-1.9%	-1.8%	-2.9%
High Income	-3.8%	-4.6%	-4.9%

Notes: The table shows the gender differential between the aggregate share of women and men with a bank account at a formal financial institution and the aggregate share of women and men who received a formal loan in the 12 months prior to the survey, every three years since 2011, for each of the developing regions of the world according to the World Bank regional classifications. High-income countries and individuals under 15 years old are excluded, except in the case of the World category and the specific high-income categories. Data come from the World Bank Global Findex Database, utilizing the regional aggregates as provided; the gender differential is calculated as the share of women with a bank account or loan minus the share of men with a bank account or loan; therefore a negative differential indicates fewer women are financially included than men, and the smaller (more negative) the differential, the larger the gender gap.

in the proportion of women and men with a bank account, in 2011 the gender gap was much wider in lower and upper middle-income countries than it was in low income countries; approximately double in both categories. However, by 2017, the order is reversed: the average gap has almost doubled in Low Income countries, which have become the income group with the widest average gap, aided in part by modest declines in the size of the gap in the two middle income categories. The reason for this is almost certainly a result of increasingly unequal growth in financial inclusion in the poorest countries; whilst overall levels of financial inclusion were low, the gap was automatically constrained, but subsequent increases in financial inclusion since 2011 have obviously been biased in favour of men. Figure 4.1 illustrates this point by plotting the average absolute shares of men and women with bank accounts in low-income countries.

From Figure 4.1 it can be seen that the overall trend in financial inclusion in the poorest countries has been positive, even in the short period of time between 2011 and 2017. The shares of both men and women with a bank account have increased considerably, with the share of women almost trebling. Despite this, however, the gap between the two lines has *widened*; this means that in the poorest countries financial inclusion has increased *more rapidly* amongst men than amongst women, and there has been a *gender bias* in the financial inclusion gains. Turning to the second panel of Table 4.1, a similar explanation likely underpins the *increases* in the size of the average gender gap in terms of access to credit in *all*

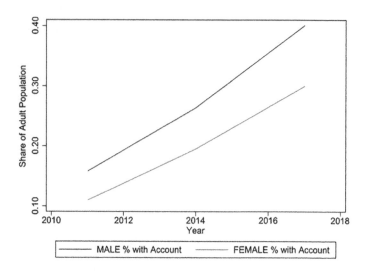

Figure 4.1   Trend in average shares of men and women with a bank
account in low income countries

income categories; as credit has become gradually more widely available across the developing world, it has done so in a manner that is biased towards male borrowers, whether via the channel of supply or of demand. This result may seem surprising given the aforementioned intense focus of microfinance institutions (MFIs) on female customers; the twofold conclusion must therefore be that (a) MFI-provided credit is still dwarfed by credit from other, non-gender-focused sources, and (b) the total number of female microfinance borrowers is not that large, at least in broad multi-country aggregates. This later conclusion is consistent with the disappointing take-up rates of many microfinance programs noted by Dahal & Fiala (2020). Note that the measure depicted only asks whether the individual had *any* formal loan within the last 12 months and does not depend on the amount, therefore microfinance loans count equally with all others.

Whilst regional and income category aggregates are very informative, it is interesting also to look at the size of the gender gap in financial inclusion in all countries of the developing world, and the spatial dispersion thereof. Figure 4.2 presents maps of Africa and Latin America with countries shaded according to the size of the gender gap in the latest 2017 round of Findex data. Figure 4.3 presents the same information for developing Asia. High-income countries are excluded, as are countries for which data are not available. The darker the shading, the wider the gender gap, although the very dark, differently shaded countries are those with either *no* or a *positive* gender gap (i.e., a higher share of women with a bank account than men). From figures 4.2 and 4.3, it can be seen that large swathes of Asia perform quite well in terms of the gender gap, although it is non-negligible in the large countries of India and China. Central Asia, some countries in the Middle East, and Bangladesh are the worst performers with extremely wide gender gaps, underlying the possible cultural element. However, Islamic-majority nations Indonesia and Kazakhstan both have positive gender gaps, so there is not an iron link between religion and gender inclusivity of the financial system. All of Africa except for Southern Africa performs quite badly in terms of the gender gap, as does much of Catholic Latin America, although there are no countries with a gender gap wider than 20 percentage points in this region. The link between conflict and the gender gap is less strong than in the case of overall financial inclusion – this is probably because conflict leads to such low levels of FI for both men and women that the gap is small by construction.

To further explore the financial inclusion gender gap, Ghosh & Vinod (2017) take a deep dive into financial access microdata in India. They first confirm the existence of the financial inclusion gender gap in India, showing that female-headed households are 8% less likely to access formal finance than households headed by males and 20% less likely to make use of cash loans. Importantly, they note also that female-headed households are 6% less likely to access *informal finance*; this finding suggests that, whilst the gender gap is smaller in informal financial inclusion, it is still present, and therefore that informal financial inclusion is not mitigating the unequal gender access of women to financial services. Section 5 goes into more detail on informal financial services, many of which are almost exclusively preponderant amongst women.

Ghosh & Vinod go on to explore the *reasons* for these observed financial inclusion gender gaps. Whilst their findings are specific to India, they serve as a useful starting point for our understanding of *why* there is

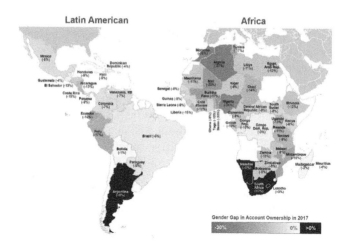

Figure 4.2   2017 width of the 'gender gap' in Latin America and Africa

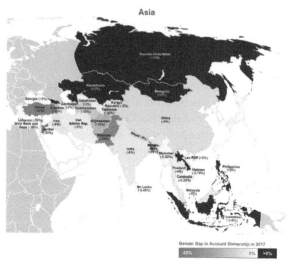

Figure 4.3   2017 width of the 'gender gap' in developing Asia

a gender gap in access to financial services. They explore various channels of discrimination against women, creating quantitative proxies for these forms of discrimination and adding interaction terms involving these proxies to their regressions to see if Indian states with higher levels of such discrimination have wider gender gaps.[2] They find that the forms of discrimination that most significantly predict a wider gender gap in financial inclusion are political discrimination, educational discrimination, and labour-market discrimination. That is, Indian states with more female representatives in the legislature, higher primary school enrolment rates of girls, and lower male–female wage differentials have on average statistically significantly smaller gender gaps in financial inclusion. The finding that it is these very practical forms of discrimination that have the biggest effect is indicative of practical rather than social drivers holding women back from accessing financial services, although of course these practical disparities may in turn trace their root cause to social factors.

Ansar et al. (2021) also note the importance of labour market factors on explaining the financial inclusion gender gap. They show from the Findex data that the gender gaps are much smaller when comparing solely *employed* males and females, implying that the gap in labour-force participation rates between men and women is a major driver of the financial inclusion differential. This kind of analysis does of course face causality issues – it may be that similar cultural factors or forms of discrimination cause the same women to be excluded from the labour market and from the banking system, rather than these women being excluded from the banking system *because* they are excluded from the labour market. Nevertheless, boosting female labour force participation, already a laudable development goal in its own right (Young 1995), may also have the additional impact of improving female financial inclusion. It is in part for this reason that many policymakers pinned such high hopes on the potential of microfinance programs to tackle both the issues of female financial exclusion, by giving access to credit, and female labour force exclusion, by facilitating entrepreneurship opportunities. It is fair to say, however, that

---

[2]   For example, ratio of men-to-women and rate of female foeticide are used as proxies of overall gender discrimination; proportion of crimes against women is used as a proxy for physical discrimination; political representation of women in the state legislature is used as a proxy for political discrimination; primary school enrolment numbers of girls is used as a proxy for educational discrimination; and the male-to-female average wage ratio is used as a proxy for labour-market discrimination.

many of these high hopes have not yet been realized (De Mel et al. 2009; Dahal & Fiala 2020). Ansar et al. (2021) also hint at some of the social factors that may be at play by noting that young women "are on average more likely than their male counterparts to report that they don't have an account because someone else in the family already has one", suggesting that lower societal emphasis on female economic autonomy may also in part drive the financial inclusion gap. The fact that, as can be seen from Table 4.1, the Middle East and North Africa is the developing region with by far the largest gender gap in financial inclusion may also reiterate this point, as this is also the region in which the highest proportion of countries still have laws in place restricting female financial autonomy (World Bank 2019). However, one must be careful in seeking a purely religious motivation for the gender gap in financial inclusion; the world's largest Islamic country, Indonesia, is also one of the few developing countries in the world where there is in fact no financial inclusion gender gap.

3.2   Why is the gender gap not closing?

The evidence presented in the above section shows that, in many developing regions, the gender gap has not closed much in the period 2011–2017, and has in some cases even widened. This may come as a surprise for at least two reasons: (1) many of the formal barriers to women accessing financial services, such as the DRC 'family code' mentioned in the introduction to this chapter, have been at least nominally removed, and (2) there has been such an explicit gender focus within financial inclusion development policy programs, especially through the microfinance channel, during this time period. The first point suggests that merely removing formal barriers is not nearly enough to redress discrimination against women in the realm of financial inclusion; as Ghosh & Vinod (2017) indicated, many of the forms of gender discrimination that drive the financial inclusion gap may be deeply structural, and will take time to work through even when formal obstacles are removed. To again paraphrase Duflo (2012), this would further indicate why specific, gender-targeted policy interventions are appropriate to speed up what can otherwise be a very slow process of increasing equality.

Regarding the second point, one explanation might be that traditional microfinance institutions or microfinance interventions have not been sufficiently broad in terms of their service offering to make a meaningful difference in attracting women to become more financially included.[3] To address this, many Microfinance Institutions are now taking a more holistic approach. Garcia & Lensink (2019) charts the transition from microfinance to 'microfinance plus', whereby financial products and services are now often bundled with trainings and other social services directed at their predominantly female clientele. These take the form both of practical business and entrepreneurship trainings, and also social assistance programs such as information and support groups around gender topics. It might be that this more holistic form of female-targeted microfinance provision will have more success in attracting higher levels of female financial inclusion, but if so it has yet to start appearing in the data. In many cases these microfinance plus programs have to compete with pre-existing female-dominated informal finance and savings clubs, many of which already offer social services to women in the form of peer-group support (Anderson & Baland 2002). Furthermore, with the Covid-19 pandemic, which had disproportionally negative effects on women and girls (UN Women 2021), the next round of Global Findex Data could yield even more sobering results. As Duflo (2012) notes, in developing country contexts, females almost always bear a higher burden from external crises, as additional resource constraints often result in further favouring of men at the societal and household levels. Therefore, it could be that the financial inclusion gender gap will be yet another example of how the Covid-19 pandemic has disproportionately negatively impacted the world's women and girls.

---

[3]   A much more optimistic assessment of the gender-equality potential of financial inclusion programs is provided by Swamy (2014); this analyses the effects of a government-mandated propagation of self-help groups linked with formal banks on local economic outcomes by gender, and found that women did indeed participate extensively in these saving and lending groups, and that these groups had a larger positive impact on localized female income growth than male. This linkage of accessible informal-style self-help groups with the established, formal banking sector may therefore represent an appealing approach both for boosting the financial inclusion of women, and achieving women empowerment outcomes, as will be discussed in Section 4.

4.   Conclusion

This chapter has told only half of the story of the complex interaction between gender and financial inclusion. The immediate issue of deep and persistent gender disparities when it comes to levels of financial inclusion is compounded by the differential nature of the way in which men and women *use* financial resources in many developing country contexts. The direct impact channel of financial inclusion on economic outcomes such as income, wealth, and consumption is therefore of critical importance when considering the gender gap – if financial inclusion leads to desirable economic outcomes, then gender disparities in financial inclusion have contributed to and entrenched gender disparities in economic enfranchisement and material wellbeing. On the flip side, if it is indeed the case that in many instances, women in developing countries use additional resources in a more sustainable and child-focused manner, then closure of the gender gap may represent *higher* marginal economic gains than those expected by merely raising the overall financial inclusion rate. Purely on the basis of the discussions in this chapter, there emerges a *triple advantage* to focusing on the financial inclusion of women. First, in many cases there is less need to overcome supply-side constraints to raise inclusion rates amongst women because the financial service providers are already there and serving men in many areas.[4] Second, by financially including women, it is possible to raise overall rates of financial inclusion and close the gender gap simultaneously – to achieve *inclusive growth* in financial inclusion. Third, as mentioned above, the *marginal gains* from financially including additional women may be greater than those achieved by financially including additional men, in terms of economic outcomes and positive economic and welfare externalities to children and wider families.[5]

---

[4]   The reverse of this is that there may be additional challenges in overcoming social and cultural constraints.

[5]   We do not of course mean to imply that there is no value in financially including more unbanked men as well. The ideal outcome would be inclusive growth via rising rates of FI amongst both men and women, with the gender gap closing as a result of a more rapid rate of inclusion amongst women as both genders approach equilibria of high rates of FI. Our purpose here is to argue that (a) women and the gender gap must not be obscured or neglected in cases where overall rates of FI are being targeted and seem to be rising; and (b) that, when development resources and FI interventions are finite and scarce, an explicit though not necessarily exclusive focus on women can yield the highest marginal gains.

Taken together, this is a powerful argument for placing women and the gender gap firmly at the centre of global FI policy and research. However, it will be seen from Chapter 5 that, once we look beyond purely economic outcomes and into the realm of women empowerment and social emancipation, this can become even a *quadruple advantage*. The most powerful arguments for the essential focus on the financial inclusion of women are still to come in the next chapter.

5. Women and financial inclusion, Part II: empowerment

1.   Introduction

In an interview conversation about the Poverty Graduation Program and subsequent research (Banerjee et al. 2015b; Banerjee et al. 2021), Nobel Prize-winning economist Abhijit Banerjee told the story of an unnamed young woman in India (Hughes 2021). This woman was a member of the 'ultra-poor'. Growing up in a village, she had been raised since birth to accept that she would be 'fully taken-care-of' by her father and then by her husband. She learned no life skills of any kind other than those of a rural housewife, and lived her life completely disconnected from the financial system or any other formal networks or social bodies. After escaping from her violently abusive husband, having long since been taken far from her paternal family unit, this young woman and her two children were left completely alone. Lacking the skills or opportunity to climb even the first rung of the ladder into any kind of work, she lived for several years in the forest on the few alms she could collect by begging, sometimes living in a tree for fear of wild animals. This was hopeless, perennial poverty – the kind of poverty where even the most meagre income was out of reach. The story ends happily, with this woman an early success story of the poverty graduation program discussed in Focus Box 3.3, having made use of the training and assets so well that she was, at the time of telling, approaching the purchase of her second house. But Professor Banerjee's purpose in telling this story was to make one important point – that even our most basic assumptions about what some women in severely patriarchal societies may have learned, may be able to do unaided, and may consider possible can regularly fail to hold. A woman with such life experience could live right next to a microfinance bank and have no idea how to make an application, or have the confidence to walk in and ask someone to explain it to her. She may not know what precisely a savings account is, let alone be able to assemble even the most meagre initial deposit to open one. The most basic forms of social interaction, commerce, and communal and business life have been shut away from her since birth.

When it comes to the young woman of this story and the tens of millions of women like her across the developing world, the route out of poverty clearly involves far more than just economic outcomes. The barriers to be overcome for her to engage in society and self-advancement at even the most basic level go far deeper and wider than financial constraints. But just as there exists a vicious circle by which lack of empowerment leads to financial exclusion leads to lack of access to financial resources and pecuniary independence leading back to further disempowerment, could there exist a virtuous circle starting with financial inclusion? Could such women find in their interactions with financial intermediaries, peer-groups, and business trainers the kind of basic social knowledge and confidence that had been deliberately kept from them throughout their upbringing? Even without a full 'big-push' of the type delivered by the poverty graduation programs of Banerjee et al. (2015b), could interventions to seek out and include such women in the financial system lead to the relaxation of these most fundamental constraints on empowerment? Even for women who do not flee or outlive their husbands, a life of complete and utter dependence on father then on husband without the most basic of social and commercial skills and experiences is clearly suboptimal – even in the most harmonious relationships, mortality rates in many developing countries are high and the risk of sudden spousal bereavement is not negligible – and many relationships are not so harmonious. With the right incentives, could the social, educational, and practical elements of well-designed financial inclusion interventions overcome these culturally imposed life-skill deficiencies for women in such a way as to also prevent obstruction from her husband because, for example, the family can access credit only through her? These are perhaps *the* most important questions surrounding the intersection of gender and financial inclusion, and the remainder of this chapter will explore them extensively.

2. Financial inclusion and women empowerment

As noted in the introduction to Chapter 4, the focus on the gender dimension of financial inclusion is not borne solely out of a desire to reduce an imbalance or inequality. There is also a widely held belief that focusing on the financial inclusion of women can achieve *additional positive outcomes* beyond merely correcting this imbalance and boosting overall financial inclusion levels by collecting the 'low-hanging fruit' of unbanked women. It is often posited that (a) women in developing country contexts utilize financial products and services differently to men, and that this different usage may be preferable from the perspective of societal welfare, and (b) that by improving the financial inclusion of women, we can achieve gains in women empowerment that go beyond the purely economic realm. This section will therefore explore the potential for such *additional societal gains* from female financial inclusion as relates to the crucially important topic of women empowerment.

2.1 Theories of financial inclusion and women empowerment

Much of the discussion of Chapter 4 focused on the potential *economic benefits* of decreasing the financial inclusion gender gap. It has been argued that, (a) by decreasing the financial inclusion gender gap, we can more easily increase rates of financial inclusion generally, thus allowing developing countries to benefit from the resulting economic gains, and (b) by focusing on increasing financial inclusion specifically of women, economic gains can be realized as a result of their differential risk and spending preferences. However, stepping outside of the purely economic realm, there is another, complementary reason to focus so specifically on increasing the financial inclusion of women – the link between financial inclusion and women empowerment.

Women empowerment of course contains an economic element, but it is much more than that. Hansen et al. (2021), following Kabeer (1999), define women empowerment as "the process through which women develop the ability to influence or take strategic decisions for their life, in contexts where this so far has been denied to them, for themselves, their families, communities, and society." This definition emphasizes the multifaceted nature of the women empowerment concept, which the authors, following Huis et al. (2017), go on to split into three strands: personal, relational, and societal empowerment. Therefore, women empowerment relates to how women feel about themselves and their personal beliefs; how women relate to and are able to bargain with others, especially within their households; and how women are able to act, and are regarded and treated, at the societal level, in terms of their ability to play a role in and influence the society around them. The important issue of *internal constraints* on women empowerment and self-advancement is discussed in detail in Focus Box 5.1. In addition to *personal, relational, and environmental (societal)* empowerment, women empowerment may also refer to *material (economic)* empowerment, commonly measured by indicators like income and/or assets.

The financial inclusion of women has the potential to contribute to driving women empowerment along all dimensions. Or, to reverse the statement, the *financial exclusion* of women has for a long time been part of the *disempowerment* of women at the personal, relational, and societal levels. By not having financial access, women do not have financial autonomy, which affects their personal empowerment. By having to depend on their fathers or husbands to make all economic decisions, because these men control the household savings accounts and access to credit, women are disempowered within their relationships. Finally, by not being able to save, borrow, and insure as equals, women are restricted in terms of their ability to function as full and equal members of society, and in terms of their ability to build the assets, capital, and influence necessary to take on societal leadership positions.

Duvendack & Mader (2020) highlight the following series of theoretical mechanisms through which female financial inclusion can impact women empowerment.[1]

1. Through financial inclusion, women can gain a larger share of control over financial resources, improving their bargaining position within a household. This can result in women wielding greater influence over household spending, family planning, and allocation of household tasks. This can also affect domestic violence, as discussed in Section 4.
2. By necessitating women to leave the home to access financial services, and to participate in business activities and transactions, women

---

[1]   This list of mechanisms has been unpicked both from the textual discussion of Duvendack & Mader (2020) and from their schematic Figure 1.

become more mobile and visible, and women feel more control over their own destinies. Societies become more accustomed to seeing women transact business and participate in commercial life.

3. Both of the above can improve the physical and mental health and wellbeing of women; and, to the extent that financial access and the subsequent business endeavours are collaborative, allow additional opportunities for the formation of female social groups, support groups and mutual solidarity, especially where the formation of such groups is an explicit component of the financial inclusion program.

4. Financial inclusion programs can be excellent opportunities to 'package in' additional social services, trainings, and support networks that spread awareness of women's rights and gender issues. Furthermore, when packaged with financial services that households want and only women can access, men are disincentivized from preventing women from attending these trainings and support services.

The next subsection will touch briefly on measurement, before section 4.4 goes on to summarize what has been discovered empirically regarding the impact of female financial inclusion on women empowerment, particularly along the lines of evidence for the mechanisms proposed in the above four-point theoretical summary.

Focus box 5.1   Internal constraints: aspirations and hope

When it comes to the link between financial inclusion and women empowerment, many of the FI interventions designed at least in part to have a positive empowerment impact often focus exclusively on relieving *external constraints*. External constraints refer to factors outside of the psyche of women and men that prevent the full agency of women: constraints such as lack of available credit, lack of safe places to store money, etc. However, development economists have increasingly started to emphasize also the importance of *internal constraints*. Internal constraints refer to psychological constraints – such as agency, mindset, hope, and aspirations – that can prevent women from attaining empowerment regardless of the availability of external tools. It is argued that interventions can only be truly transformative when the impact of internal constraints is also taken into account (Duflo 2012, 2013; Genicot & Ray 2017; Garcia et al. 2020). If internal constraints are binding, standard economic interventions may not work regardless of how effectively they relax external constraints. For example, providing women with access to credit will be of no value if her aspirations and sense of self-worth are sufficiently constrained that she has no confidence to make use of it. Research has shown that women in developing country contexts often suffer from mindset constraints leading them to be more risk-averse and less entrepreneurial than men, sometimes to a suboptimal degree (Siba 2019). A particularly notable example of such an internal constraint manifesting into a real-world decision-set constraint is the *home bias* amongst female entrepreneurs uncovered by Said et al. (2021), whereby a rigorous RCT in Pakistan uncovered that, whilst financial inclusion in the form of credit access and business training boosted entrepreneurial activity amongst women, these women displayed a strong preference only to start businesses based in their own homes. Furthermore, they displayed a strong preference for taking financial advice from male partners over outsiders, even when these outsiders were more qualified. These two factors, attributed by the authors to the internalization of gender-norms, severely limited the sustainability and scope for expansion of women-owned microenterprises. In order to combat this, it is important that policy interventions address internal constraints alongside the external, resulting in policies that have multiple dimensions.

Policy approaches to relieving internal constraints by improving hopes and aspirations have taken multiple forms: for example, by exposing individuals to role models (Beaman et al. 2012; Bernard et al. 2015, 2019; Riley 2017; Cecchi et al. 2021), or by stimulating interactions with peers (Dasgupta et al. 2015; Field et al. 2016). Some development interventions have included a dimension specifically designed to relieve internal constraints. An excellent recent example is Bossuroy et al. (2021), who discusses the impact of a multi-faceted social protection program in Niger, where an internal constraint intervention (a psycho-social intervention) is combined with a package of other interventions, including savings promotion, an entrepreneurship training, and a cash transfer. In line with the Poverty Graduation Program discussed in Focus Box 3.3, it appears that a full package of interventions can be very successful. However, the study also strongly highlights the positive effects of addressing internal psychological constraints. In other cases, certain types of policy intervention may relieve internal constraints automatically. Garcia et al. (2020) show that membership of microfinance institutions may automatically boost aspirations because of the peer effects of participating in borrower groups, demonstrating that, although internal constraints were often not a specific focus of microfinance interventions, they may in practice have been relieved anyway. The successful accidental effects of prior policy interventions on relieving internal constraints can greatly aid in informing intentional effects of interventions going forward. By enhancing aspirations, it may not just be that constraints *preventing* women from benefiting from opportunities for empowerment and self-improvement are removed. Interventions that enhance aspirations may even generate a so-called aspirations gap – a gap between what people aspire to and what they have now – that may incentivize individuals to take actions to narrow it (Ray, 2006; Lybbert & Wydick 2018), thereby creating an additional *positive incentive* for women to improve their material and societal situation. Accounting for internal constraints can therefore both boost the potential gains from the relaxation of external constraints and generate positive economic and empowerment outcomes in their own right.

2.2   Measuring women empowerment

Before going on to explore the empirical evidence around the effects of financial inclusion on women empowerment, it is necessary to briefly highlight some of the issues around *measuring* women empowerment, and how these issues can be overcome. If we are to have any hope of evaluating impacts of financial inclusion policies and programs on women empowerment, we first need a clear and consistent framework for measuring it as an outcome variable, and also for understanding which aspects of empowerment may *not* be captured by our measures, and therefore the inherent limitations of any studies that employ them.

As the concept of women empowerment is broad and multifaceted, including bargaining power, freedom of movement, access to resources, and feelings of agency (Huis et al. 2020), measuring women empowerment is far from straightforward. Glennerster et al. (2019) discuss the essence of the challenge by noting that most women empowerment concepts centre on agency and choice, and that the individual *decision-making process* is something that is rarely directly observed, even when the choice *outcomes* are. Whilst individuals can be asked directly about their decision-making via surveys and questionnaires, such surveys are fraught with all manner of reporting biases.[2] In order to alleviate these potential biases, in addition to standard survey-based measures it is vital to integrate non-survey instruments to measure women empowerment. Examples of these can include list randomizations, behavioural games, and vignettes. The paper by Bulte & Lensink (2019) discussed extensively in Section 4 shows how dramatically results can change when direct survey-reporting biases are properly accounted for.

Different approaches to measuring a similar dimension of women empowerment may lead to diverging results, which complicates a correct measurement of women empowerment even further. Moreover, different dimensions of women empowerment may be negatively correlated with each other. For instance, recent work emphasizes that women's higher income-generating capacity, and human capital accumulation relative to men, whilst enhancing the *economic empowerment* of women, may induce a male backlash effect and consequently an increase in intimate partner violence (Bulte & Lensink 2019). Such conflicts are often observed between *personal empowerment* and *relational empowerment*, as men resist and react negatively to the personal empowerment gains of women. Glennerster et al. (2019) also note that women empowerment is a continuous and multi-stage process, and therefore that measurement must incorporate these different stages. Similar to the Duvendack & Mader (2020) division between lower-order and higher-order outcomes, it is stated that measuring impacts on women empowerment holistically requires careful selection and measurement of short-term, intermediate, and final outcomes, alongside means of identifying the causal links between them. "For instance, say we want to measure whether a negotiation program empowers girls to complete secondary school. We will need to measure their resources (such as their negotiation ability), the decision-making process between parents and girls that determines whether they stay in school, and their ultimate educational achievement" (Glennerster et al. 2019, p. 7). Finally, it is noted that, as women empowerment involves many different concepts and elements, it is difficult to (a)

---

2   For example, social desirability bias, which "occurs when respondents give answers that they think the surveyor wants to hear or that are in line with generally accepted social norms rather than reality" can often lead to overly optimistic portrays of the state of women empowerment, especially when assessed around sensitive issues such as domestic violence (Glennerster et al. 2019, p. 7).

prioritize, and (b) formulate outcome measures that are simultaneously specific enough to capture contextual nuance whilst general enough to be comparable across contexts. This final point is similar to one of the major difficulties in measuring financial inclusion discussed in Chapter 1: when a concept has a variety of different outcome measures covering a plethora of different elements, it is difficult to objectively establish and rank *overall* levels, be it of financial inclusion or of women empowerment. The challenge therefore multiplies when one is simultaneously evaluating both of these concepts!

In order to properly measure women empowerment, we therefore need to select measures that capture (a) the personal, relational, societal, and purely economic elements, (b) the short-term, intermediate, and final outcomes, and (c) the elements of agency and decision-making without suffering from reporting bias. To do all of these things together is an almost insurmountable challenge. Many papers and evaluations therefore choose to focus on a specific subset of these elements and outcomes. For example, Huis et al. (2020) draw from the psychology literature to formulate measures of women's self-esteem on the basis of the Rosenberg (1965) scale; this involves asking a series of positive and negative questions with answers on a 1 (strongly disagree) to 5 (strongly agree) scale, the answers of which can then be aggregated into an overall index measure of self-esteem. This measure relates to the *personal* element of women empowerment. However, the same paper also focuses on the *relational* element by additionally asking questions about intimate partner violence and creating a measure based on whether women had experienced *at least one form* of such violence in the previous six months, and by utilizing a standardized scale of intra-household decision-making (Mizan 1993), which asks women who in their household takes the lead role in a series of different common household decisions, and then aggregating the results into a single scale. Especially the latter index, based on a series of questions related to women's role in household decisions, is commonly used by economists as a proxy for women's bargaining power in the family (Angelucci et al. 2015; Banerjee et al. 2015a). There are also several examples of multi-dimensional measures of women empowerment, such as the Women's Empowerment in Agriculture Index (WEAI) (Alkire et al. 2013), which is a validated multi-dimensional measure of women empowerment, and measures of anthropometry and food security.

Glennerster et al. (2019) provide a *measurement strategy* for evaluating women empowerment, whereby a four-point plan is proposed for building such measures. The plan is as follows, although it is stressed that the steps may need to take place simultaneously and exhibit some overlap, rather than being purely consecutive:

1. conduct formative research to understand gender and empowerment in the specific context;
2. map a theory of change and use it to select appropriate outcomes and indicators;
3. develop and validate data collection instruments that minimize reporting bias;
4. design a data collection plan that minimizes measurement error.

By utilizing this measurement strategy, one can systematically address most of the different elements, outcomes, and challenges of women empowerment measurement outlined above, and use the *context* and accompanying *theory* to guide the decisions over which indicators to prioritize and select. This strategy is by design highly context specific and will therefore yield a body of women empowerment research that is diverse in terms of its measures and mechanisms, but such a varied body of research is fundamentally necessary for widely evaluating such an intangible and multi-faceted concept.

2.3   The impacts of financial inclusion on women empowerment

We are now in a position to examine some of the empirical evidence regarding the impact of financial inclusion on women empowerment established thus far. It may seem that the concepts and measures of this body of research vary greatly, but this is for the reasons established in the discussion of the women empowerment measurement strategy of Glennerster et al. (2019); whilst the concept remains multi-faceted and non-static, and whilst the contexts vary both in terms of settings and of policy interventions, the measures and outcomes of individual studies will necessarily vary. It is then the role of meta-analyses and systematic reviews of reviews to combine and aggregate these individual findings, such as the review of reviews by Duvendack & Mader (2020).

The overall conclusion of Duvendack & Mader is quite positive, with the authors noting, "meta-analysis findings for women's empowerment appear to be generally positive", and "the effects of financial services on women's empowerment seem to be an exception from the mixed picture, with generally positive outcomes recorded by most meta-studies" (p. 615), the 'mixed picture' being the somewhat sombre overall finding of the review of reviews that many financial inclusion programs failed or underperformed in terms of more general (non-gendered) outcomes. The authors do, however, add the following notes of caution:

1. whilst the impacts of financial inclusion programs on gendered and women empowerment outcomes are usually positive, these impacts are sometimes quite small in overall magnitude;
2. often, these positive women empowerment effects are more likely attributed to the *non-financial program features*, such as the afore-mentioned trainings and support groups, rather than the increases in financial access and inclusion themselves;
3. the findings of positive effects "were highly dependent on how empowerment was conceptualized and measured, which was not consistent across studies" (Duvendack & Mader 2020, p. 615).

This latter point may be less of an issue given the discussion of female empowerment measurement in the previous subsection. As empowerment concepts differ depending on context, positive impacts across a variety of different empowerment indicators may in fact be more reassuring than if a smaller number of more standardized and homogenous outcome measures were employed. It would, however, be more of a problem if the same interventions were having null or even negative effects on women empowerment when alternative measures were used. The severity of the first and second concern is fairly subjective: effects may be small, but if they are there, at least the general direction of the theoretical mechanisms seems to hold, and the task of the policymakers can then be either how to increase the magnitude of the efficacy of these already-positive interventions, or how to combine different interventions so as to multiply the effects. It is, however, important that the *cost of interventions* is taken into account; expensive programs with positive but small impacts might not be optimal uses of finite supplies of development aid resources. Similarly, the second concern depends very much on whether (a) it is believed that these non-financial program features can be delivered without the financial inclusion shell, and (b) whether the financial elements have additional impacts beyond women empowerment. Indeed it may be a problem if otherwise unsuccessful financial inclusion programs are used as inefficient delivery mechanisms for trainings and support groups that could be provided anyway; however, if financial inclusion programs are having positive effects more generally, than the ability to add a positive gender component by adding on such additional elements can add further positive effects, and this can only be a good thing, especially in scenarios where women would likely be socially prohibited from attending such trainings and support groups without the financial incentive.

Moving now from the general to the specific, having seen that the *overall* effect of financial inclusion programs on women empowerment is believed to be positive, let us now examine the empirical effects of specific financial inclusion interventions. These are, specifically, financial and microfinance interventions such as provision of credit, savings, and insurance products; non-financial interventions such as trainings and support groups; and market-based financial inclusion products such as mobile money.

2.3.1   Credit

Generally speaking, the provision of credit to women was expected to yield positive impacts on economic outcomes, even when compared with provision of credit to men, because women were believed to be more credit constrained, and therefore unable to take advantage of a wider array of profit-making opportunities because of lack of credit (Pitt & Khandker 1998). Additionally, the provision of credit to women was expected to yield a positive *women empowerment impact*, by giving women a larger share in the control of overall household resources, thereby improving their intra-household bargaining position (Mayoux 1999; Guérin et al. 2010; Kulkarni 2011), and by integrating women more deeply into the world beyond their home through their interactions with the microfinance organization, their business interactions around utilizing the funds, and their interactions as part of a borrowing group when the loans were group based (Hansen et al. 2021).

The results surrounding the economic impacts on women of these microcredit programs are at best mixed, with many RCT-based studies reporting either no or very modest overall gains of microcredit on long-term economic outcomes, gains that did not seem to greatly improve when the focus was specifically on women (Banerjee et al. 2015a; Tarozzi et al. 2015). One important study even found that economic effects were *less positive* for women than men, although this intervention was a cash transfer/gift rather than a repayable loan (De Mel et al. 2009), and the explanation likely came from additional societal constraints on women. The explanation for these muted findings might be low take-up rates of the offered loans (Dahal & Fiala 2020); given that these loans are often targeted specifically at women, it may be that societal pressures or constraints, or merely internalized feelings of disempowerment, restrict women's ability or confidence to take out loans even when they are available. A more positive finding of Swamy (2014) suggests a large positive impact of financial self-help groups linked with formal banks on women's incomes in India, differentially so as compared with men; however, this was not exactly a microfinance or microcredit intervention in the traditional sense. Another interesting study, also focusing on self-help groups developed under India's National Rural Livelihoods program, shows theoretically and empirically that only large loans will lead to better bargaining power of women within their households (Kochar et al. 2022). The question of who controls household resources only becomes important if the loan amount is large enough. This study therefore provides a potential explanation for why many microcredit programs do not show large positive impacts on women's bargaining power: the loan is simply too small. A similar explanation is posited in Section 6 for why small economic gains from the financial inclusion of women fail to reduce levels of intimate partner violence, and may in fact increase it.

If provision of microfinance has often failed to yield positive economic outcomes for women, and especially if this failure is down to low take-up rates, then one might expect also to see disappointing impacts on women empowerment, especially as one of the key mechanisms relies on women having control over a larger share of household resources (Vaessen et al. 2014). Despite this, there is some evidence of positive effects. A variety of papers that have utilized survey measures of personal and relational women empowerment, such as the above-discussed psychological measures of Huis et al. (2020), have reported *positive causal increases* in personal and relational empowerment of female microcredit borrowers as compared to non-borrowers (Pitt et al. 2006; Basargekar 2009; Kato & Kratzer 2013; Hansen 2015). The key to reconciling these differences in economic outcomes and women empowerment outcomes may be take-up rates; if take-up rates are low, the small number of women who *do* utilize the microcredit might see both income and personal and relational empowerment gains, but the number of such women may be too small as to detect a positive effect at the aggregate level. The major papers that showed no *economic* effect of microcredit programs on women also showed no *empowerment effect* (Banerjee et al. 2015a; Crépon et al. 2015; Tarozzi et al. 2015), although these tended to measure empowerment purely along the dimension of intra-household bargaining.

There are also even some papers that have developed theoretical mechanisms and accompanying empirical evidence for a *disempowerment effect* of microcredit on women. These also follow the essence of the earlier-mentioned cautionary guidance of Koczberski (1998) that in developing country contexts, piling more work and responsibilities on women can often lead to more overburdening. Added to the physical burden of any additional work required as a result of utilizing the borrowed funds can be the psychological burden of the outstanding repayments, especially if the loan is in the woman's name but her husband still controls most of the household income and expenditure streams (Garikipati 2008). Furthermore, increased control of household resources can come at the cost of increased intimate-partner violence, either if the man attempts to use violence as a means to influence how the woman will utilize *her* resources (Ahmed 2005), or if the man feels emasculated by being frozen out of microcredit access and uses violence as a way to 'redress the balance' from his own perspective (Pratto and Walker 2004). Sometimes, an increase in violence or abuse towards women who become visibly involved in microcredit transactions can even extend to the wider community (Rahman 1999). Therefore, it is crucially important that any researcher or policymaker be aware of the fact that interventions can have *precisely the opposite* impact on women empowerment than was expected and desired, and that, when this impact involves violence, the result of an insufficiently developed policy or research strategy can be devastating.

In summary, the evidence surrounding the impact of microcredit on women empowerment is mixed at best and concerning at worst, and it would certainly appear that microcredit, possibly as a result of low take-up rates, has thus far had no more than a peripheral impact on women empowerment beyond empowerment at the most personal level.

2.3.2   Savings

Despite the fact that 'secure saving facilities' may appear to be the most basic and simple of financial products, provision of saving services was not initially a major part of microfinance programs – perhaps indeed because it was seen as *too simple* to have any latent demand. Despite this, the fact that women so heavily participate in informal savings clubs, and that women have so actively embraced even fairly simple mobile money services (Suri & Jack 2016) suggests that *there was and there remains a latent demand from women for secure savings services.*[3]

Drawing from the empirical literature around these informal savings clubs, we can glean some insight as to the mechanisms by which greater access to savings facilities may positively impact women empowerment. Anderson & Baland (2002) provide evidence that a major reason women participate in informal savings clubs is to *protect* their savings from capture by their husbands and other friends and family. Furthermore, their findings indicate that, when women do manage to save a specific amount for a specific purpose, their husbands are much more open to spending the money in the way the woman intended. This suggests a *direct impact* on female control over the use of her own savings and resources from the availability of secure saving facilities. Schaner (2017) underscores the results by Anderson& Baland (2002) by providing evidence that intrahousehold issues explain demand for financial products. More in particular, she shows that reducing withdrawal fees may have perverse effects when bargaining power is low. Relatedly, Dongen et al. (2022), in a study on savings by Pakistan women, show that only women with substantial bargaining power actively use newly opened savings accounts. A study based in the Philippines (Ashraf et al. 2010) attempted to formalize the kind of 'commitment saving' offered by the informal savings clubs by offering a very limited access savings account through a local microbank, which also yielded a positive impact on the control women exercised over the use of the funds when they mature. Karlan et al. (2017) also confirmed the positive impacts on women empowerment of informal savings groups across a variety of different African settings.

---

[3] Of course, women utilize savings clubs for other reasons than actual savings, such as social interactions and as a form of insurance. Despite this, the fact that Dupas & Robinson (2013a) found a demand for *additional savings products* within the informal savings club (ROSCA) framework suggests that a latent demand for saving facilities is indeed still present within the membership of such clubs.

In terms of the economic impact of micro-savings for women, Dupas & Robinson (2013b) not only discovered a *positive* impact of savings accounts on economic outcomes for women in Kenya, but failed to find such an impact for men, providing evidence that the *latent demand* for quality savings facilities is likely greater amongst women than men. The study gave non-interest-bearing bank accounts with hefty withdrawal fees, which act as a commitment device, both to randomly allocated (mostly female) market vendors and to (mostly male) bicycle taxi drivers. Access to the accounts causally increased savings levels (a first-order effect) and then productive investments and expenditures (a second-order effect) amongst the market traders, but not the taxi drivers. Of course, part of the difference is likely due to the different investment opportunities available in the two different careers, but this would not explain the first-order effect of increased saving. It is interesting that this relatively simple, very basic savings account yielded positive economic impacts that many more complex microcredit products could not, suggesting that the early micro-finance policymakers may have erred in their assumptions about where the latent demand amongst women lay; it was assumed that women were credit constrained, but maybe they were in fact more constrained merely in terms of safe places to save their money, not least from their husbands.

2.3.3   Insurance

Whilst insurance has been seen as an increasingly important financial inclusion product for some time now, it has often been prioritized more on the basis of economic activity than of gender (Casaburi & Willis 2018; Belissa et al. 2019). This is because smoothening adverse climatic shocks to the agricultural sector has been thought of as the area where low-level insurance products might do the greatest marginal good. However, a large amount of women are involved in agricultural production, and so will often have access to these insurance products. Hill et al. (2013) suggest women in developing countries are more risk averse than men; this was already noted as one of the explanations why microcredit providers often prioritize women, because they are expected to be more careful with the funds, but should also indicate that insurance products should be more attractive to female as opposed to male entrepreneurs. Evaluations of specific, female-targeted insurance are thus far quite scarce, but as the range of products and services offered by microfinance institutions broadens, the opportunities to evaluate the specific gender and women empowerment effects of insurance may arise.

2.3.4 Transfers; and cash transfers

Like savings, the ability to make safe and low-cost financial transfers is another financial service that may for some time have been thought of as too basic to warrant serious inclusion into the package of microfinance products offered. Yet, the ability to make transfers *independently* may actually have non-negligible impacts on female financial autonomy and women empowerment. In many developing countries, money is still often transferred by hand as cash; for example, when a family need to make a transfer to a neighbouring village, they wait until a trusted friend or relative is travelling that way and ask them to physically carry the money. This kind of physical cash transfer has become far less common following the advent of mobile money, but there are still many countries in Sub-Saharan Africa where mobile money has yet to really take hold (Hinson et al. 2019). It can easily be imagined that, when cash has to be transferred in this cumbersome and unsafe way, male family members take the lead, and with it the control. It also may be the case that automatic transfer systems can make repayments of loans easier, therefore relieving some of the aforementioned additional burden and pressure that responsibility over microcredit access may inadvertently place on women (Garikipati 2008).

Transfers as a financial inclusion product can refer not only to the ability to make transfers, but also to the provision of cash transfers in the form of grants or gifts. In this case, women are given money directly with the hope that it will facilitate their financial autonomy or advance their independent businesses or micro-enterprises. Such cash transfers are a key feature of the De Mel et al. (2009) paper, which has been frequently discussed in this chapter. The transfers themselves are perhaps not a financial inclusion product *per se*. However, they can be used as a means to boost financial inclusion alongside other aims: for example, if women are issued with a new bank account into which cash grants are deposited, they become 'banked' and also must become accustomed to using the account in order to access the funds. Similarly, even though in practice cash transfers can be spent on anything, theories of fly-paper effects and the non-fungibility of government benefits suggest that often if people are allocated grants for a specific purpose, they will spend at least a proportion of them on that purpose (Inman 2009; Hastings & Shapiro 2013). Casaburi & Willis (2018) showed that cash gifts given to farmers immediately before offering them the chance to buy an insurance product were often spent on the insurance product. Therefore, cash transfers with the stated intention of facilitating financial inclusion or stimulating microenterprises or investment opportunities may indeed end up being used for these purposes.

2.4 Non-financial interventions

Whilst it might seem strange to talk about 'non-financial interventions' in a book about financial inclusion, it is often the case that trainings, support groups, and information sessions can be thought of as aspects of financial inclusion policy, especially when (a) the trainings or information sessions contain components related to entrepreneurship training, financial literacy, or business training; or (b) when the non-financial interventions are packaged alongside financial products and services, either because it is believed they will be mutually complementary, or because by thus packaging these products it might be easier for women to gain the blessing of husbands or male family members to utilize the non-financial services. Indeed, it has already been noted that the Duvendack & Mader (2020) review of reviews places much of the credit for the positive impacts of financial inclusion on women empowerment outcomes on the non-financial intervention components of financial inclusion projects and programs.

The most obvious form of training that can be offered as a financial inclusion project is business and/or entrepreneurship training. The idea is that, by simultaneously offering women access to credit and training as to how to optimally invest in and develop a microenterprise, they have the best chance of generating positive economic and empowerment outcomes from this increased financial access. An additional women empowerment effect may be observed if this increases women's overall confidence in making decisions independent and proactively. Bulte et al. (2017) examined the impact of offering female-targeted business trainings through an existing microfinance bank in Vietnam and find positive effects of the training on profits and business entry and exit; Huis et al. (2020) find positive female empowerment effects of the same intervention. However, Bulte & Lensink (2019), again focusing on the same intervention, provides a cautionary tale regarding the impact business and gender training on intimate-partner violence. Hansen (2015) also finds a positive female empowerment effect, especially on the societal empowerment dimension, of a similar but longer-term business training intervention in Sri Lanka.

McKenzie & Woodruff (2013), by contrast, conduct a meta-analysis of business trainings packaged with financial inclusion products around the world and find that, in most cases, the impacts are small and dissipate rapidly for recipients of either gender. The aforementioned De Mel et al. (2009) study even finds positive impacts for men but not for women, although these may be due more to the cash transfer itself than the business training that accompanied it. However, some other more recent papers with a more explicit focus on the training element reach similar conclusions (Berge et al. 2015; Giné and Mansuri 2021).

Instead of or in addition to business trainings, some financial inclusion programs prefer to package-in 'social trainings' such as discussions of gender issues, women's rights, or formation of support groups or services specifically for women. These trainings may still be business related, such as focusing on the specific challenges faced by women in business, or may focus entirely on other gender and empowerment topics. A third of the training in the aforementioned Bulte et al. (2017) study was gender rather than business related, although whilst the study found a positive overall economic impact of the training, it is not possible to disentangle the separate effects of the business and gender training components. Huis et al (2020), however, when examining the empowerment effects of the same intervention, were able to isolate most of the positive causal effect on women empowerment to the gender-topics component of the training. Adoho et al. (2014), when evaluating the impact of a vocational training specifically targeted at adolescent girls and young women in Liberia, with a strong empowerment component, found positive impacts on both economic and empowerment outcomes.

The outstanding questions surrounding these 'non-financial interventions' relate not only to their efficacy but also to the extent to which they *need* be packaged alongside more traditional financial inclusion projects and products. The trainings themselves are often relatively cheap, meaning that even findings of modest impacts may be quite attractive from a cost–benefit perspective. On the one hand, adding an inexpensive training to a much more expensive financial outreach project may seem like a relatively easy add-on and improvement; on the other, if the inexpensive training outperforms the costly finance intervention on women empowerment outcomes, this may point to a fundamental imbalance of priorities. Going forward, more research is needed into precisely disentangling the separate contributions of financial interventions and different types of non-financial interventions on women empowerment outcomes, so as to better ascertain the degree to which they depend upon each other.

2.5   Market-based interventions

The final type of financial inclusion interventions that may affect women empowerment outcomes are what we will broadly refer to as 'market-based interventions'. In principle, we use this term to refer to any specific financial product or service that is designed, at least in part, to boost financial inclusion, but which stems entirely from the realm of the private financial sector for profit-driven motives, rather than from either international development policymakers or local governments. For example, whilst Burgess & Pande (2005) and Swamy (2014) analyse the impacts of the opening of rural private bank branches or bank-linked support groups, these are not considered market-based interventions because they were mandated by governments specifically because private banks were not doing them independently. In practice, the market-based financial inclusion interventions fall into two categories: (1) deliberate attempts to capture unbanked customers by opening branches or offering services in previously underserved areas, such as the Equity Bank of Kenya business strategy discussed in Focus Box 1.1, and (2) the advent and proliferation of mobile money services and other forms of FinTech (Hinson et al. 2019).

Of course, because of the nature of these private sector advances, there is rarely an explicit focus on gender, and women empowerment is not the primary goal. Nevertheless, it can be very interesting to assess the gender-specific *impacts* of these new advances, services, and technologies. The Allen at al. (2021) paper does not explicitly examine the gendered impacts. However, it is demonstrated through their controls that women have a statistically significantly lower probability of holding a bank account in under-served areas prior to the rollout of targeted Equity Bank branches in 2006, and therefore presumably benefitted at least as much as men from the improved financial access spurred by this private bank expansion, if not more. If some of the above-discussed evidence regarding the latent demand amongst women for savings products and safe financial transfer facilities is accurate, private banks may in the future find that it is profitable to specifically target women in the same manner that Equity Bank specifically targeted unbanked rural dwellers and ethnic minorities.

When it comes to analysing the gendered impact of mobile money, the key paper has already featured a few times throughout this chapter: Suri & Jack (2016). This paper examines the entirety of the roll-out of the Kenyan Mobile Money system M-PESA and, utilizing a clever identification strategy based on exogenous changes in access as the system was gradually rolled out across different geographic areas, uncovers a significant positive impact of access to mobile money on household consumption levels overall, but *especially and of greater magnitude* on female-headed households. Higher consumption is an effective proxy for higher economic wellbeing and standards of living. This is an excellent example of how an empirical paper was able to capture both lower- and higher-order outcomes and the channel between them: the finding of increased levels of financial inclusion via the utilization of the mobile money services is the lower-order outcome of the M-PESA roll-out, and the subsequent finding of increased household consumption levels, especially within female-headed households, which causally followed from the utilization of mobile money services is the higher-order outcome.

By showing the effect of mobile money access on consumption across the full income distribution of both male- and female-headed households, Suri & Jack shed further light on the mechanics of the positive impact on female-headed households. They find that the strongest effect is on the *bottom half* of the income distribution of female-headed households, indicating that the gains are concentrated amongst the poorest women. Additionally, the fact that overall consumption growth was negative for these households suggests a mechanism: "the primary impact on female-headed households was therefore to protect them from falls in consumption in the longer term, or to boost it marginally." In other words, mobile money acted as a form of financial safety net for female-headed households, both in terms of creating buffer savings and facilitating easier requests for remittances in bad times, which supports some of the previous theoretical arguments regarding the positive effects of female financial inclusion on female financial autonomy and self-determination. Further mechanisms were uncovered in that the mobile money access allowed women to reduce multiple income streams and therefore specialize, and to move from subsistence agriculture to 'business or sales'-related activities both on the intensive and extensive margin. This also supports the theoretical expectation of female financial inclusion leading to both positive economic and women empowerment outcomes via the entrepreneurship channel, whilst bypassing the Koczberski (1998) caution against overburdening women by reducing their burden in the sphere of subsistence agriculture.

It is telling that, in this chapter, some of the most positive measurable impacts of female financial inclusion on economic and empowerment outcomes come from the market-based intervention of mobile money rather than many of the aforementioned microfinance and development policy initiatives. At the same time, in the realm of gender equality, there are clear boundaries on the potential of the private sector alone to yield optimal results. Whilst economic impacts on women are important, much of this chapter has concerned itself with intangible concepts of equality and women empowerment, which are unlikely ever to be a top priority of private sector profit-driven initiatives. The Duflo (2012) prescription still remains: if we want to see rapid gains in women empowerment, we must focus policy specifically on women empowerment, rather than merely sitting back and expecting it to arise organically through other channels.

3.   Women and informal finance

Much of the research and policy focus on financial inclusion is concerned exclusively with access to *formal* finance. However, the story of women and financial inclusion is not complete without some consideration of informal finance, as informal financial services are often disproportionately utilized by women, and because, whilst a 'second-best' option when compared with non-exploitative formal financial products, they often represent a considerable improvement on the scenario with no access to financial services of any kind. Whilst overrepresentation of women in many informal financial transactions is seemingly insufficient to fully mitigate the gender gap in formal finance (Ghosh & Vinod 2017), it may still be that positive informal financial arrangements alleviate some of the negative impacts of formal financial exclusion on women and women empowerment. On the other hand, exploitative informal finance may be yet another burden that unbanked women and girls have to navigate.

We propose that informal financial services in developing countries can be concisely categorized in the following manner: unilateral arrangements, bilateral arrangements, and multilateral arrangements. Generally speaking, the former has the largest potential for exploitation and abuse, and the latter the largest potential for economic and social empowerment. Unilateral arrangements refer to 'take it or leave it' offers from informal moneylenders; sometimes at exploitative rates of interest, and sometimes involving disproportionate collateral deposits. In some cases, female borrowers from informal moneylenders can face additional exploitation in the form of sexual coercion (ILO 2014). Removing women from the influence of such predatory moneylenders can therefore be a large additional women empowerment gain of formal financial inclusion. Nevertheless, there are some scenarios where even unilateral informal moneylending need not be exploitative and is in fact welfare enhancing. For example, Ghosh et al. (2001) present a theoretical model where asymmetric information in the forms of adverse selection and moral hazard lead to credit rationing from formal moneylenders. To the extent that informal moneylenders have better local knowledge or local monitoring capacity than formal lenders, they may in fact be able to charge lower rates of interest or offer loans of a larger size (Madestam 2014). The fact that women are seen as more trustworthy may also see them benefit from lower rates than men from informal moneylenders.

Bilateral arrangements refer to informal financial arrangements made more collaboratively between the borrower and lender, but still involving just those two parties. Linked transactions are a common example of bilateral informal financial arrangements; for example, where landowners or contractors provide the credit to tenants or contract farmers to buy seed and fertilizer at planting time, and collect the outstanding balance in the form of a share of the crops, or an exclusive arrangement to buy the crops at a prespecified price, at harvest time (Casaburi & Willis 2018). These may be fairly neutral in terms of both exploitation and gender impact, although of course some negative features of unilateral informal finance may still be present. Finally, multilateral arrangements refer to informal group or club arrangements, where many people come together to join informal financial associations.

This latter form of informal finance is of particular relevance to the gender aspect of financial inclusion for two reasons: (1) because such clubs are very heavily dominated by female members, and are often exclusively female (Anderson & Baland 2002; Dupas & Robinson 2013a); and (2) because these groups provide social networks and support groups by their very existence, which may have a positive impact especially on the societal dimension of women empowerment. Additionally, they may provide women with business connections leading to opportunities for economic empowerment. The most common form of such multilateral informal financial services groups are rotating savings and credit associations (ROSCAs). ROSCAs are informal clubs, where all participants are expected to make regular small contributions in exchange for occasional large payouts. In other words, small contributions are pooled and paid out to different members in turn, although in some cases the pay-out recipients can instead be selected randomly. These forms of ROSCAs are therefore essentially savings clubs, where small contributions are made in expectation of a large payout at a future date that is usually known in advance. Other credit- or insurance-based ROSCAs make the large payouts to recipients on the basis of need, either as a loan to be repaid to the group or as an emergency transfer.

Anderson & Baland (2002) explores the nature of ROSCAs in depth, first constructing general theoretical models to explain why women choose to join such clubs, and then testing the predictions of these models on data from ROSCAs in the slums of Kenya. They first confirm the fact that membership of ROSCAs in the Kenyan context is almost exclusively female, and that these women are usually living in couples, but with independent income streams. Their theoretical models suggest, "participation in a ROSCA is a strategy a wife employs to protect her savings against claims by her husband for immediate consumption", which explains the popularity of ROSCAs amongst income-earning women with husbands or partners. The model assumes that women have a higher preference for saving than their partners, that their share of household bargaining power is less, and that therefore when their income is unprotected, less will be saved than they would like. It predicts that it is suboptimal for women with particularly high levels of bargaining power to save in ROSCAs, as they can allocate funds closer to their preferences anyway, and for women with particularly low levels of bargaining power to save in ROSCAs, as it is likely that even the full ROSCA payout will be seized by the husband. However, due to the decreasing marginal utility of the husband for transient consumption, for women with intermediate levels of bargaining power, a single large pay-out can be allocated more according to her preference than a continuous stream of small pay-outs. Anderson & Baland explore this hypothesis on data from Kenyan ROSCAs, and find that the effect of women's household bargaining power, as proxied by their household income share, does indeed follow the expected inverted-U shape pattern in terms of probability of ROSCA membership. That is, probability of joining a ROSCA is increasing in household income share up to a turning point, and then decreasing thereafter.

Such informal savings associations are very common across the developing world, and insights such as the above into *why* women form and join such groups can be very illuminating in terms of the relationship between women and financial services. For example, the fact that access to savings products seem to have stronger women empowerment impacts than access to credit, as highlighted in the previous section, can be explained in this way. Similarly, such findings of the need to protect resources from partners inform the aforementioned De Mel et al. (2008) explanation for why female entrepreneurs were able to use cash transfers less productively. The more successful network effects of ROSCAs can also be seen as inspiration for the construction of formal savings groups or group borrowing facilities. In all, informal lending remains a second-best solution behind fair formal financial access; however, as an intermediate step, the right kinds of informal financial associations often arise organically and can alleviate some of the welfare losses from financial exclusion. Similarly, the construction of financial products and services that women in developing countries *actually want to use* can be greatly informed by studying and unpacking the popular informal financial products and services.

4.   Financial inclusion and domestic violence

Of all forms of women disempowerment, physical intimate partner violence is perhaps the most horrible and the most damaging. The tragic concept of 'missing women' (Sen 1992) refers to the deficit of women in substantial parts of Asia and North Africa, compared with how the female-to-male ratio should be in biological expectation, and is due in large part to both deficiencies in the relative care of female children, and the disproportionate levels of violent acts against adult women. Intimate partner, or domestic, violence has a profound negative impact on all forms of women empowerment: it damages personal empowerment by affecting how women feel about themselves; it damages relational empowerment by providing a threat that reduces the bargaining power of women in relationships; and it damages societal empowerment by restricting the ability of women to move and operate freely outside of the home without fear of repercussions. If the financial inclusion of women has the potential to reduce the levels of domestic violence to which women are subjected, this could be one of the most powerful women empowerment outcomes of closing the gender gap (Farmer & Tiefenthaler 1997). On the other hand, according to some theoretical and empirical research (Anderberg & Rainer 2011; Bulte & Lensink 2019), there are certain contexts and scenarios in which financial inclusion programs can actually *increase* levels of domestic violence. Even more worryingly, standard survey approaches to program impact evaluation can often fail to detect this effect. Therefore, the potential domestic violence impact of any and all financial inclusion policy inventions should be one of the most paramount concerns to any policymaker.

To speak of domestic violence through the prism of economic utility theory may seem cold and uncomfortable to many readers. However, in order to properly understand the impacts of economic programs on domestic violence, it is necessary to cast the problem of domestic violence within an economic framework. Domestic violence is an abhorrent phenomenon, and the purpose of theorizing about it is in no way to normalize or justify it, but merely to understand how to reduce it from a practical perspective. There are two major theories of domestic abuse: expressive violence theory, and instrumental violence theory. In expressive violence theory, violence enters directly into the utility function of the perpetrator as it gives him some positive utility as an expression of dominance, a conformity to social norms, or some other perspective (Farmer & Tiefenthaler 1997). In instrumental violence theory, the male perpetrator uses violence as a bargaining tool to exert control over scare household resources (Anderberg & Rainer 2011). In both cases, men cannot push the violence too far: if the disutility to women of suffering the violence becomes greater than the disutility of leaving or divorcing their partner – the 'outside option' – then they might leave, in turn causing disutility to the male perpetrator. Therefore, the level of domestic violence is constrained by the possibility of divorce, and the extent of this constraint depends on the difficulties and social stigma associated with divorce in the specific societal contexts.

In expressive violence theory, increasing the financial autonomy or income levels of women, for instance by improving financial inclusion, reduces the level of domestic violence, because it reduces the cost of the 'outside option'. If women have independent resources, or capacity to generate income streams, it is easier for them to leave violent partners either temporarily or permanently. Knowing this, violent partners will reduce the level of violence. According to this theory, there is unlikely to be a harmful impact of increasing financial inclusion of women on levels of domestic violence. However, in the case of instrumental violence theory, the picture is more complicated. The relationship between the financial autonomy or income levels of women and domestic violence becomes non-monotonic. This is because men use violence to gain control of the resources of women, or to influence their decisions as to how to allocate their resources. When female partners have very low income levels, or low levels of financial autonomy, violence levels will be lower because there are only a few resources for the men to take. As women start to earn more, or have access to more funds because, for example, only women can access microfinance programs in that area, the level of violence actually *increases*, because now there are more resources for the man to take from the woman. This pattern will be observed up to a certain threshold point, after which the income level or financial autonomy level of the woman is so great that the man must reduce the level of violence, because otherwise his partner can afford to leave him. Therefore, when women have low income levels or levels of financial inclusion, domestic violence may *increase* as financial inclusion increases, until that level becomes sufficiently high that violence starts to decrease again. Focus Box 5.2 discusses in greater depth the theoretical background to the interaction between female financial inclusion and violence, and presents a theoretical model of this troubling phenomenon. It bears repeating at this point that there is no acceptable 'level' of domestic violence, and framing such violence in terms of utility and rationality does not imply that the perpetrators are acting in a manner that is in any way acceptable; it is merely a tool for understanding how incomes, financial inclusion, and violence interact so as to best act in the interests of women by reducing or eliminating such violence.

In empirical terms, assessing the effect of financial inclusion programs, or indeed of any policy interventions, on domestic violence is more challenging than on many other outcomes. This is because domestic violence is a very sensitive topic, and standard survey methods and measures may fail to elicit true responses from both women and men. Bulte & Lensink (2019) illustrate this point when evaluating the impact on domestic violence of a combined business and gender topics training in rural Vietnam. This study focused on already entrepreneurial women, by selecting only micro-enterprise owners as participants. The context of rural Vietnam is one in which divorce is very uncommon and there is much social stigma attached to divorcees; therefore, the 'outside option' for women is very expensive and the authors were concerned about the possibility of the positive economic outcomes generated by the entrepreneurship training leading to higher levels of domestic abuse through the mechanism of instrumental violence. In order to evaluate the effect on domestic violence, the authors measured the level of domestic violence suffered by the treatment group who received the training, as compared with the control group who did not. They measured this in two ways; both by a direct survey method (asking direct questions about the levels of domestic abuse to which women were subjected), and via list experiments, which is a specific survey technique designed to elicit true responses to sensitive questions. The method works by presenting the respondent with a series of statements, and asking how many they agree with; most are neutral statements, and one is a sensitive statement about the level of domestic violence. A control group receive only the neutral statements. The difference in the average number of 'yes' responses between the treatment and control groups then yields an estimate of the total proportion of respondents who answered yes to the sensitive statement; in this case, that they were subjected to domestic violence. More details of the list experiment method can be found in Blair & Imai (2012).

Bulte & Lensink concluded, on the basis of the list experiment, that the gender and entrepreneurship training had actually *increased* the levels of domestic violence endured by participants as compared with non-participants. An additional paper on the same program (Bulte et al. 2017) also showed that the program had successfully increased the economic outcomes of the female participants, leading to the possibility that the increased levels of domestic violence were due to the increased incomes of the women. Perhaps more importantly, on the basis of the direct survey method, the impact on domestic violence was the *exact opposite*. When asked directly, the women who received the training self-reported lower levels of domestic violence than the non-participants. Had the researchers simply used the direct survey technique, they would have falsely concluded that the FI program had both increased female incomes and reduced domestic violence, and the evaluation would have been unequivocally positive. This goes to illustrate two critical points: (1) that it *is* possible for financial inclusion of women to *increase* levels of domestic violence in certain cases and contexts; and (2) that in the absence of sophisticated techniques for eliciting true responses, these effects may not show up in program evaluations and may even appear to operate in the opposite direction.

Going forward, it can be seen that the complicated picture emerging from both the theory and empirics linking domestic violence and financial inclusion leads to a very difficult trade-off for policymakers. Any increase in domestic violence is terrible and must be avoided at all costs. However, if fears of increasing domestic violence prevent policymakers from implementing programs that may boost the incomes and levels of financial inclusion of women, this is just another manifestation of how perpetrators can use violence to restrict the opportunities and empowerment of women. Two possible solutions present themselves. First, even in the instrumental violence theories, when the increase in female income and financial autonomy is sufficiently large, levels of violence reduce. Therefore, it is optimal to focus on interventions with large impacts. This can be easier said than done, however; throughout previous chapters it has been shown that FI interventions often have smaller positive impacts than are expected. Second, by decreasing the cost of the outside option, the ability of men to use violence as an instrument of control is reduced. Therefore, specific financial aid to single or divorced women, support groups designed around helping women through the process of divorce or separation, or context-specific drives to reduce the stigma attached to divorce, may all have the potential to mitigate any violence-increasing effects of financial inclusion programs. However, as has been shown throughout this discussion, the implementation of such things is easier said than done, and when the safety of women is at stake, there is no room for error.

Focus box 5.2   **A theoretical model on financial inclusion and intimate partner violence[4]**

This focus box presents a simple theoretical model to show that programs to empower women, including programs that aim to improve financial inclusion, may invite a male backlash and increase intimate partner violence (IPV). We will show that this may especially be the case in societies where divorce is stigmatized.

---

[4]   This focus box is based on Bulte & Lensink (2020).

The model rests on assumptions that may be debated: alternative models, with different implications, are available (e.g., Eswaran & Malhotra 2011). The main aim is to show that improving financial inclusion of women may have counterintuitive negative effects on IPV, and to analyse under which conditions these negative effects are more likely to materialize.

We assume a simple model with homogenous match quality. Spouses pool part of their income in a "common pot" to finance household public goods, and use remaining funds in line with their own preferences. In patriarchal cultures with strong gender roles, the husband decides about the contribution share or family tax rate, $\theta \varepsilon$ [0,1] (Malapit 2012). Spousal income is given (and observable) and both partners contribute equal shares of their endowment to the common pot. The husband chooses the contribution level that maximizes his private payoffs, or the sum of benefits from consuming household good G and his post-tax discretionary income. Hence:

$$\pi_h = \delta_h \mu G(\cdot) + (1 - \delta_h)(1 - \theta_h) Y_h \quad (1)$$

where π_h denotes the husband's payoffs, δ_h is a parameter ($0 < \delta < 1$) capturing the husband's preferences for household good $G(\cdot)$ financed via the common pot, and Y_h is the husband's income. We assume that parameter μ, $0 < \mu < 1$, is a measure of male bargaining power (or social empowerment) that is exogenous to the household. It affects how much the husband captures of the household good (in case of a divisible good such as food), or the extent to which good G reflects his preferences – as opposed to his wife's. The first term of (1) represents the husband's utility from the household good, and the second describes utility of his residual income.

Assume that couples can produce household goods more effectively than singles. One extreme assumption is that production satisfies $G(\theta_h Y_h, \theta_w Y_w) \geq 0; G(0, \theta_w Y_w) = G(\theta_h Y_h, 0) = 0$, or that household goods can only be produced by couples (where Y_w denotes the wife's income). The Cobb–Douglas production function satisfies these restrictions:

$$G(\theta_h Y_h, \theta_w Y_w) = A(\theta_h Y_h)^\alpha (\theta_w Y_w)^\beta \quad (2)$$

where A is a production parameter. We also assume $\alpha + \beta < 1$, or decreasing returns to scale in the production of household goods. The husband's optimal contribution share is:

$$\theta_h^* = \left[\frac{(\alpha + \beta)\delta_h \mu A Y_w^\beta}{(1 - \delta_h) Y_h^{1-\alpha}} \right]^{1/(1-\alpha-\beta)} \tag{3}$$

The condition shows that share θ_h^* is *increasing* in male bargaining power and female income. If women are socially disempowered, the husband enjoys a greater share of the household good, and higher female income leverages his ability to "free ride" on his wife to fund the household good. Assume the wife's objective function is similar, but her level of bargaining power equals $(1-\mu)$, and she has a different taste parameter δ_w. If she could choose the contribution level, she would choose:

$$\theta_w^* = \left[\frac{(\alpha + \beta)\delta_w (1 - \mu) A Y_h^\alpha}{(1 - \delta_w) Y_w^{1-\beta}} \right]^{1/(1-\alpha-\beta)} \tag{4}$$

Observe that the wife's optimal contribution share is *decreasing* in male bargaining power and her own income. It is evident why intra-household conflict may emerge. This happens if preferences diverge, $\delta_h \neq \delta_w$, if spouses earn different incomes, $Y_h \neq Y_w$, or when the bargaining power is unequal, $\mu \neq 1/2$. The husband demands a higher contribution than his wife prefers to pay if:

$$\frac{\mu}{1-\mu} > \frac{Y_h}{Y_w} \frac{\beta \delta_w (1 - \delta_h)}{\delta_h (1 - \delta_w)} \left(\frac{\alpha^\alpha}{\alpha + \beta} \right)^{1/(1-\alpha)} \tag{5}$$

We assume husbands can use violence to discipline their unwilling wives, forcing them to contribute $\theta_h^* Y_w$ to the common pot, if $\theta_h^* > \theta_w^*$. To simplify the exposition, we assume the utility loss of abuse to the wife is proportional to the intensity of violence, or the gap in preferred contribution levels: $\gamma \left(\theta_h^* - \theta_w^* \right)$.

Solving the model

The household violence model is solved using backward induction. In the final stage, the wife decides whether to abandon her husband or stay married. The cost of divorce is context specific. In societies where divorced women are social outcasts, the reservation level of utility is close to zero, implying wives have few options but to stay married (and possibly endure extensive abuse, as in Bloch and Rao 2002). In other settings, women can leave their husband without excessive stigma costs. Upon divorce, a woman loses access to the joint household good but spends her full income on private goods, so her participation constraint is:

$$\delta_w(1-\mu)G(\cdot)+(1-\delta_w)(1-\theta)Y_w-\gamma\left(\theta_h^*-\theta_w^*(\cdot)\right)\geq(1-\delta_w)Y_w-S$$

(6)

where S captures the (society-specific) utility loss caused by stigmatization. Rearranging terms gives the following constraint:

$$\left(\delta_w(1-\mu)AY_h^\alpha Y_w^\beta\right)\theta_h^{\alpha+\beta}\geq\left((1-\delta_w)Y_w+\gamma\right)\theta-\gamma\theta_w^*(\cdot)-S$$

(7)

This can be solved for critical contribution level $\widehat{\theta}_h$ where the wife is indifferent between marriage and divorce. If husbands demand a contribution share exceeding $\widehat{\theta}_h$, the wife is better off abandoning him. This equilibrium is unique (for $\alpha+\beta<1$).[5] Note we also know the following:[6]

---

[5]   This can easily be shown graphically. Imagine a figure with contribution share θ on the horizontal axis. The term on the LHS of (7) is a concave function starting from the origin, and the sum of terms on the RHS is a straight line with negative intercept $(-\gamma\theta_w^*-S)$ and positive slope $\left((1-\delta_w)Y_w+\gamma\right)$. These lines will cross once.

[6]   Write the participation constraint as $v\widehat{\theta}^{\alpha+\beta}+\sigma\widehat{\theta}+\tau=0$, with $v>0$, $\sigma<0$ and $\tau>0$. Taking total differentials of this condition immediately yields:

$$\frac{d\widehat{\theta}}{da}<0,\ \frac{d\widehat{\theta}}{d\sigma}<0\ \text{and}\ \frac{d\widehat{\theta}}{d\tau}<0.$$ From these conditions follows (8).

$$\frac{d\hat{\theta}}{d(1-\mu)} > 0 \text{ and } \frac{d\hat{\theta}}{dY_w} > < 0 \qquad (8)$$

The sign of the first term follows because empowered women enjoy a greater share of the household goods, and are willing to pay a larger share of their income (so that the intensity of violence decreases). Both effects imply women are better off, enabling the husband to increase the contribution share – bringing his wife back to her reservation utility. The sign of the second term is more complex: (1) higher female income increases the supply of household goods, but (2) her preferred contribution level shifts down (intensifying conflict) and (3) her reservation utility level increases. The net effect on the threshold $\hat{\theta}_h$ is ambiguous. Women empowerment, stigmatization of divorce, and intimate partner violence

We can now characterize how different types of interventions aimed to improve women empowerment may affect domestic violence. We distinguish between an intervention that focuses on changing social norms, for example changing traditional gender norms. This intervention implies promoting norms of gender equity, and hence will lower μ, which we will name social empowerment. The other intervention we consider is an economic empowerment intervention, aiming to raise female income (Y_w), which we will refer by economic empowerment.

Two types of equilibria may materialize:

Case 1: $\theta_h^* < \hat{\theta}$. The husband's preferred contribution level is below the critical contribution level, so he sets his preferred rate as defined by (3). This case may especially be relevant in a context where divorce is difficult or impossible (because of stigma). IPV is determined by the gap between the preferred contribution levels: $\gamma\left(\theta_h^* - \theta_w^*\right)$.

Result 1a: For 'interior solution' $\theta = \theta_h^* < \hat{\theta}$, social empowerment lowers the contribution level set by the husband, and increases the optimal contribution level of the wife. The level of IPV goes down:

$$\left(\frac{d\theta_h^*}{d(1-\mu)} < 0; \frac{d\theta_w^*}{d(1-\mu)} > 0\right).$$

Result 1b: For 'interior solution' $\theta = \theta_h^* < \hat{\theta}$, economic empowerment raises the contribution level set by the husband and decreases the wife's optimal contribution level, so the level of IPV increases:

$$\left(\frac{d\theta_h^*}{dY_w} > 0; \frac{d\theta_w^*}{dY_w} < 0 \right).$$

Case 2: $\theta_h^* > \hat{\theta}$. The husband's preferred contribution level exceeds the threshold as defined by the participation constraint. This case may especially be important in a context where divorce does not invite strong stigma effects. Assuming the husband prefers to stay married (he can always earn the same payoffs as under divorce by setting $\theta = 0$), his optimal response is to set $\theta = \hat{\theta}$, so the relevant comparative statics follow directly from (8).

Result 2a: For 'corner solution' $\theta = \hat{\theta}$, social empowerment shifts up the critical contribution level, which increases the level of IPV:

$$\left(\frac{d\hat{\theta}}{d(1-\mu)} > 0 \right).$$

Result 2b: For 'corner solution' $\theta = \hat{\theta}$, economic empowerment ambiguously affects the critical contribution level and the level of violence.

Financial inclusion and IPV

The above analyses clearly suggest that the impact of women empowerment interventions on the prevalence of IPV varies with local conditions, in particular the interplay between stigma of divorce and pre-existing levels of income and gender equity. Moreover, whilst increasing female bargaining power and income are both important dimensions of female empowerment, the theory predicts these are distinct concepts with (possibly) opposing impacts on IPV. The analysis also suggests that empowerment interventions should be tailored to local conditions to avoid male backlash.

The analyses also provide insights on the potential impact of financially including women on IPV. Financial inclusion may improve female income (economic empowerment) as well as female bargaining power (social empowerment). The analyses suggest that in countries where divorce is difficult, social empowerment of women will lower

IPV, while economic empowerment will increase IPV. Conversely, in a context where divorce does not invite strong stigma effects, social empowerment of women will increase IPV, and the impact of economic empowerment is a priori ambiguous. The ultimate impact of financial inclusion on IPV depends on the relative strength of the bargaining power effect versus the income effect, as well as the local conditions.

As the bargaining power effect of financial inclusion will probably be of second order, that is, it will not materialise before income has been improved, it is likely that the income effect will surpass the bargaining power effect. The implication then may be that, especially in countries where divorce is stigmatized, improving financial inclusion of women will invite more IPV.

5. Conclusions

From the various discussions laid out in this chapter and that which preceded it, it will now be apparent that the gender dimension is not just an offshoot of financial inclusion research and development policy, but is at the very core. Even before the 'gender gap' was quantified, and closing it became a major policy priority, there was a continual understanding of the need to focus microfinance products and other FI interventions predominantly on women and girls. The persistence of the gender gap, and the failure of policy to narrow it in many countries and geographic regions, is not only testament to the stubbornness of both formal and informal gender discrimination across the world, but also an inditement of the fact that many FI interventions *have not* succeeded for women in a hugely meaningful way, either as a result of low take-up rates, ineffectual programs, co-optation of funds by fathers and husbands, or social and societal contexts that prevent women making optimal use of such opportunities.

Despite this, the story of gendered financial inclusion is not entirely one of failure. In many cases, more simple financial products such as secure savings facilities and the ability to make rapid and safe transfers have yielded strongly and disproportionately positive economic outcomes for women, even when more complex credit or insurance products have not. Given the preference for such basic financial services amongst the largely female informal finance self-help groups and savings associations, this should perhaps be not so surprising, and suggests the benefit of development policymakers allowing themselves to be guided in the construction of formal financial products by the demands of these informal groups. Similarly, the fact that market-based financial inclusion products and services such as mobile money have yielded meaningful impacts for women again shows that both the latent demand and economic potential is there if the product is right.

Perhaps most importantly, the link between financial inclusion and women empowerment, whilst complex and multifaceted, has repeatedly been established across a large number of societal contexts and empowerment dimensions. The finding of positive effects of financial inclusion and financial autonomy across a range of women empowerment measures is becoming an established empirical regularity and, whilst the magnitude of the effects varies and are sometimes smaller than may have been hoped in advance, the consistency in these findings should at least give hope to researchers and policymakers. Improving the magnitude or intensity of something that already works is surely a less daunting task than going back to the drawing board on projects and interventions that do not work at all. Nevertheless, the dimensions of women empowerment do not always improve symbiotically and, on many occasions, there may actually be tension between, for example, personal and economic empowerment with empowerment and relationships. This tension manifests in the worst possible way when economic gains for women lead to a 'male backlash' in terms of domestic violence, and cases such as these point to the extreme level of care that must be taken in properly developing and evaluating gendered financial inclusion interventions.

Going forward, whilst the 'gender gap' remains stubbornly persistent, there is an ever-pressing demand for further research both into why this gap is failing to close, and what can be done to close it. It appears that successful new financial inclusion products can be better informed by paying closer attention to where there is latent demand: for example, which products and services are women trying to develop for themselves in informal groups? Similarly, by packaging products together in innovative ways, there may be better potential to unpick the societal constraints on women achieving greater economic autonomy, and maybe even on relieving internal constraints, which are perhaps the most pernicious of all. How to combine financial and non-financial interventions, and development policy with market-based products, in addition to evaluating which facets of combined products are more integral than others, will likely form a large part of the future of gendered FI interventions and experiments in the field; doing so may not only have a multiplicative effect in terms of the economic impacts, but also may allow for multiple women empowerment dimensions to be improved in symbiosis rather than in conflict.

6. Financial inclusion: FinTech and the future

1.   Introduction

In May 2010 a man in Florida, USA purchased two pizzas for 10,000 bitcoin. Widely considered the first ever cryptocurrency transaction, it would have been hard to predict at the time that just over eleven years later bitcoin would officially become legal tender in a sovereign state. But technology and innovation is inherently unpredictable, and in September 2021 the developing country of El Salvador became the first nation to not only designate bitcoin as legal tender, but obligate businesses to accept it for transactions, as well as allowing taxes, subsidies, and public fees to be settled in the digital currency (Zagorsky 2021). We will not comment on the wider implications of this decision by the Salvadorian government, save to say that it is controversial. However, this example serves to illustrate how rapidly new financial technologies – FinTech – can take hold, and how they can play a sudden and unexpected new role in the world of financial inclusion.

As part of the bitcoin rollout in El Salvador, every citizen was given the opportunity to open a bitcoin 'digital wallet' – the cryptocurrency equivalent of a bank account – via a new government-sponsored app. These wallets came loaded with a government transfer of the amount of bitcoin that traded at $30 US[1] at the launch-day market price. Bitcoin ATMs were installed such that wallet-holders could withdraw their digital currency

---

[1]   Approximately 0.75% of Salvadorian GDP per capita in current US dollars at the time of the launch.

in US dollars cash, or deposit cash to buy bitcoin.[2] Additionally, the government subsidized transaction fees such that remittances from abroad could be received via bitcoin at negligible cost. Within just one month of the rollout, almost 50% of the Salvadorian population had downloaded the digital wallet, compared with only 29% of Salvadorians holding bank accounts according to the last (2017) round of Findex data. Think about how remarkable that is. If – and it is an if – one considers the bitcoin digital wallet to be equivalent to a bank account, this relatively new technology has banked more Salvadorians in a month than the conventional banking system did in its entire history.

We do not claim that it is *because* it was bitcoin or cryptocurrency that such a remarkable uptake was observed; quite probably a government transfer of dollars requiring the download of a simple online banking app would have had the same result. Furthermore, we have commented repeatedly in previous chapters on the important difference between 'access to' and 'use of' financial services, and it remains to be seen how many Salvadorians will continue to use their digital wallets once the initial transfer has been depleted. But what is clearly the case is that it was *technological innovation* that facilitated this remarkable result. Without the technology to provide virtual banking services via apps, to put those services into the hands of individuals via relatively low-cost mobile phones, to keep them safe and secure, and to maintain internet connectivity such that individuals can actually access and use their digital accounts across the country, rapid new forms of financial inclusion of this type would not be viable. This serves to indicate both the power of technological change to influence financial inclusion, the unpredictability of it, and some of the basic technological conditions necessary for a country to be able to take advantage of it.

This concluding chapter will remain relatively short, as we are now exploring the frontier of financial products and services and their accompanying FI implications. The empirical research is limited, and in many ways the future of FinTech in the developing world is still unpredictable.

---

2   It is important to note that El Salvador is a dollarized country, meaning that it uses the US dollar as official currency and legal tender. In adopting bitcoin, therefore, El Salvador did not give up precedence of its own currency but instead added the 'private currency' of bitcoin to the foreign currency it was already using in place of domestic currency.

Nevertheless, the reader should leave this chapter with at least some idea of the direction in which research into FinTech and financial inclusion is heading, and may indeed be inspired with some ideas for research of their own.

2.   Definitions and history

The general definition of 'FinTech' becomes quickly apparent merely by restating the concept in its unabbreviated form – financial technologies. However, all financial products and services utilize technology in some form or another, and traditional banking has been largely electronic for decades (although the 'electronicification' of financial sectors may have occurred much later in many developing and particularly African countries). In contemporary parlance, there is something distinctively modern, digital, novel, and innovative about FinTech (Philippon 2016; Zavolokina et al. 2016). FinTech involves companies utilizing innovation within the dynamic and rapidly evolving digital world to develop new technologies for use in the provision of financial products and services, or even in the creation of new such products and services (Navaretti et al. 2017). The reason why this digital world offers such scope for new technologies is not just its dynamism and the fact that it has been for some years a magnet for innovation and investment, but also because of the nature of its output. FinTech products and services are inherently scaleable,[3] and the business model is such that the platforms are often free at the point of delivery to the end users. This makes them potentially very appropriate for rolling out to developing country markets where the marginal benefits of expanding to additional customers is quite low in terms of revenues, and the customers themselves are unlikely to be willing or able to bear much burden in terms of costs and fees. This comes with concomitant advantages for financial inclusivity: if the marginal costs of expanding FinTech services to new customers are lower than those of conventional

---

[3]   That is, once the initial fixed costs of developing the technologies, which often come in the form of apps or websites or at worst small pin-point terminals, are incurred, the variable costs of distributing them widely can be vanishingly small. The downside is that these are also ripe conditions for the establishment of monopolies and market power for those which can afford to overcome the barriers to entry which the high initial fixed costs imply.

banking or even of microfinance, many previously financially excluded individuals may now become viable clients. Of course, many of these technologies come with the considerable downside of extensive electronic and digital infrastructure requirements at both the national (in terms of reliable energy grids) and individual (in terms of internet subscriptions and phone-handsets) levels (Demirgüç-Kunt et al. 2018), which act as an opposite push factor in their ability to boost financial inclusion.

Whilst many FinTechs remain almost exclusively confined to developed countries in terms of any degree of serious market penetration (Yermack 2018), looking briefly at the global evolution of FinTech and the FinTech sector in recent years may provide some optimism in terms of the way things are going. Arner et al. (2015) conceptualize Fintech as a new name for an old sector and discuss FinTechs as an evolution of changes in technologically enabled financial innovations over time. This discussion yields a chronological typography of the eras of FinTech beginning in the heart of the industrial revolution period. The first period, 1866–1967, is described as FinTech 1.0 and took place exclusively in the developed world. This period is characterized by the gradual establishment of remote financial services via telegraph networks, which expanded internationally across the developed world as trans-Atlantic and inter-European telegraph cables were laid, and facilitated the introduction of the first credit cards and charge cards. FinTech 2.0 is then dated to have begun around 1967 and rolled into the early 21st century, with the digitization of the financial sector in developed and then developing countries leading to ATM networks, electronic stock exchanges, and later internet banking. This era was more global, especially following the advent of the internet, although large swathes of developing countries did not have sufficient infrastructural capabilities to participate. Already between eras 1.0 and 2.0, the beginning of two trends can be observed: (1) the ability of technology to increase the *speed* and *distance* of financial transactions, and (2) the reduction of costs at the point of sale, as ATMs represented cheaper retail nodes than branches, and internet banking represented cheaper retail nodes than ATMs. Both of these trends are obviously conducive for financial inclusion.

Arner et al. (2015) then argue that the early 21st century represents a new era – FinTech 3.0. This era is characterized by technology no longer serving exclusively existing financial service providers and allowing conventional banks to disperse their products and services more widely and rapidly, but by a *democratization* of the financial technology field. That is, FinTech 3.0 actually facilitates new and different entrants to the market via the internet, mobile platforms, and digital start-up culture. The driving force behind this era is claimed to be a rapid global decline in trust in conventional banking institutions following the Global Financial Crisis of 2008. The serendipity of this exogenous shock to trust occurring just when digital technology had evolved to such an extent that new entrants could easily deliver products and services via websites and phones, directly or with fewer intermediaries, meant that citizens were willing to shift to these new providers on a large scale. And just as the declines in trust were global, so is this FinTech era – although Arner et al. distinguish between 'FinTech 3.0' and '3.5', the latter of which they demark as the developing world element. The difference between the two is that 3.5 is more inherently low-fi, and does not presuppose for example the wide dispersion of smartphones, instead evolving around these constraints by the development of, for example, mobile money. But equally important is a willingness of developing country *governments* and *regulators* to be more receptive to these new technologies. Whilst developed country markets and regulations tended to be already open and to adapt in tandem with new FinTechs, developing countries were often more resistant and protective of existing market structures. FinTech 3.5 therefore is characterized also by a shift in attitudes, and accompanying market reforms, such that now in many cases developing countries are actually *more* receptive to new and alternative financial technologies. El Salvador acting as a cryptocurrency pioneer is an example of this. Therefore, whilst the current numbers over the global dispersion of many FinTechs – mobile money excluded – may inspire pessimism from a developing country perspective, the evolution of the eras of FinTech is much more optimistic in terms of the future direction and potential beneficiaries of these technologies.

3.   Mobile money

3.1   Adoption and penetration of mobile money

When discussing new technologies in the realm of financial inclusion and development, there is one clear starting point in terms of both market penetration and transformative potential. Mobile money can be defined as financial products and services bought and utilized using purely a cellphone, and which have expanded to include a wide range of financial services including not just storing, borrowing, and transferring money, but also business services, insurance, and investment products (Hinson et al. 2019). A relatively new phenomenon, mobile money has emerged organically as a result of technological advances in cellphone software and hardware,[4] and has been driven predominantly by banks and financial institutions within Sub-Saharan Africa rather than by external international organizations (Allen et al. 2014). Particularly in East Africa, mobile money has taken a strong foothold in the financial sector, and is expanding across the continent.

It is easy to assume that mobile money in the developing world is the preserve of the wealthy, or the middle class, because it requires the capital asset of a cellphone. In fact, it is *not necessary* to own a smartphone in order to hold a mobile money account and to perform basic mobile money transactions. A simple Nokia (or equivalent) handset is sufficient, such as can be purchased across the developing world for a few dollars, or even less in the second-hand market. In fact, to hold a mobile money account you need only a SIM card, although you would have to borrow a phone from a friend or neighbour in order to insert the SIM card to make a transaction. Neither do you need 4G or 3G coverage, nor the technological skills to install and navigate an app – basic mobile money transactions can be performed with cellphone menu codes and SMSs through the conventional 2G cellphone network. Furthermore, you do not even need to own a phone or a SIM card *to make use* of mobile money. Suri & Jack (2016), a key paper in understanding the scale and impacts of mobile money services in East Africa that featured heavily in Chapter 4, goes into some detail about the system of *agents* in providing mobile money services. This system is key to the identification strategy of the paper. Mobile money agents are the 'retail arm' of the mobile banking system, and they require nothing more than a cellphone and a small cash

---

[4]   Whilst software advances in systems and encryption were of course crucial to safe adoption of mobile banking, the most important advance has been the decreasing cost of cellphone and smartphone ownership resulting from technological progress in electronics manufacturing. A prerequisite to an effective mobile banking system is a large proportion of cellphone ownership within the population, and decreased costs alongside increased knowledge have led to booms in cellphone ownership since 2000 in many African countries (Pew Research Centre 2015).

float.[5] These agents earn small commissions by performing transactions on behalf of people around them using their own phone or mobile money accounts and collecting or dispensing cash in exchange. Therefore, whilst it is not possible to be a mobile money account holder without a phone or SIM card, it is still possible to access and use mobile money services by visiting one of these numerous agents. As the overheads and fixed costs for agents are extremely low, they are much more widely dispersed than conventional bank or even MFI outlets and can operate in small and isolated locations provided there is basic cellular phone service (Aron 2018).

Mobile money services arose with little fanfare but have seemingly had very promising results in terms of 'catching on' with developing country populations and providing access to basic financial services – financial inclusion. Allen at al. (2014) show that not only has the use of mobile phones to access financial services rapidly taken off in Sub-Saharan Africa, it has done so much more extensively than in other developing regions. Formal analysis of whether expanded mobile banking boosts financial inclusion is somewhat redundant; if one accepts a 'mobile wallet', as at least in part equivalent to a bank account, the positive effect on financial inclusion is automatic. Whilst Allen et al. caution that the range of financial products and services accessed with cellphones was smaller than those at conventional banks during the period of their sample up to 2009, Hinson et al. (2019) note the later broadening of the range of mobile financial services, in addition to discussing the positive economic effects of these trends on agribusinesses. Table 6.1 presents an overview of the depth of mobile money penetration in the major developing regions from the most recent round of Findex data in 2017, although mobile money services are expanding so rapidly in some countries that the latest 2017 data are surely already out of date. As the proliferation of mobile money is so new, questions regarding its usage were only included in the more recent rounds of Findex surveys, and therefore it is not possible to examine evolution over time. The upper panel of Table 6.1 shows the share of adult individuals with a mobile money account, the lower panel shows the share of *total domestic remittances* that were received using a mobile phone.

---

5   Although usually mobile money agents operate out of an existing shop or premises, or within a small booth sponsored by, and emblazoned with advertising for, the mobile money provider (Aron 2018).

From Table 6.1, it can immediately be seen that mobile money really is a Sub-Saharan African (SSA) phenomenon. In both the upper and lower panels, we observe a clear 'SSA gap' – but this time, the gap is positively skewed in favour of SSA. That is, SSA has a higher mobile money penetration than other developing regions both in terms of accounts holders, whereby it is the only developing region in which account ownership is even in double figures, and in terms of share of total remittances, where, with the exception of East Asia and the Pacific, share of remittances received via mobile phones in other developing regions are less than half of those of SSA. The right-hand side of Table 6.1 shows the mobile money penetration statistics for the three highest and lowest SSA countries for each indicator.[6] It can be seen that, even within the region of SSA, there is great between-country disparity in the degree of mobile money penetration.

The founding[7] East African Community (EAC) countries clearly lead the way in terms of mobile money adoption. Indeed, Kenya has the highest share of mobile money account holders in its population of any country in the world, with Uganda second. Some major economies of West Africa are not far behind, with the share of population with a mobile money account reaching 39% in Ghana and 34% in Cote d'Ivoire in 2017. The 11 countries in the world with the highest share of mobile money account holders were all in Sub-Saharan Africa,[8] and only three of the top 20 are outside this region. Despite this, many Sub-Saharan African countries still have low or even negligible degrees of mobile money adoption. It can be seen from Table 6.1 that Mauritania and especially Ethiopia perform badly on both indicators. Figure 6.1 illustrates the degree of mobile money account ownership across the continent of Africa.

From Figure 6.1, the geographic disparities in mobile money penetration across SSA can be clearly observed. High or healthy adoption rates in the East African Community, Southern Africa, and the more developed countries of West Africa contrast strongly with low rates in Central

---

[6]   Of the countries for which detailed Findex data is available. It is likely that, in the countries for which these data are not available, mobile money penetration may be lower than that of Ethiopia.

[7]   South Sudan ascended to the EAC in 2016 and, in contrast with fellow members, remains one of the lowest-performing African states in terms of mobile money penetration.

[8]   The 12th was Paraguay; only three of the top 20 are not in SSA.

Table 6.1   Aggregate mobile money penetration in 2017 in the developing world

Men and women

*Share of 15+ Individuals who **have a mobile money account***

	2017		2017
East Asia & Pacific	1%	Kenya	73%
Europe & Central Asia	3%	Uganda	51%
Latin America & Caribbean	5%	Zimbabwe	49%
Middle East and North Africa	6%	Nigeria	6%
South Asia	4%	Mauritania	4%
Sub-Saharan Africa	21%	Ethiopia.	<1%

*Share of **total domestic remittances** received with a mobile phone*

	2017		2017
East Asia & Pacific	40%	Kenya	94%
Europe & Central Asia	21%	Tanzania	89%
Latin America & Caribbean	12%	Uganda	82%
Middle East and North Africa	1%	South Sudan	11%
South Asia	11%	Mauritania	8%
Sub-Saharan Africa	48%	Ethiopia*	1%

Notes: The upper table shows the aggregate share of individuals with a mobile money account, while the lower table shows the shares of total domestic remittances that are received via a mobile phone. The left-hand side shows the data for each of the developing regions of the world according to the World Bank regional classifications; the right-hand side shows the data for the highest- and lowest-performing Sub-Saharan African countries for each indicator. High-income countries and individuals under 15 years old are excluded. Data come from the World Bank Global Findex Database utilizing the regional aggregates as provided.
* Of the countries for which detailed Findex data are available. It is likely that, in the countries for which these data are not available, the mobile money penetration may be lower than that of Ethiopia.

Africa, the Guinea Coast, and the countries of the Saharan belt. In general, formerly British colonies exhibit quite high levels of mobile money penetration, with the notable exception of Nigeria. Yermack (2018) discusses the correlations between legal, constitutional, and institutional history

Figure 6.1   2017 levels of mobile money penetration in
             Sub-Saharan Africa

and FinTech penetration in an argument similar to that discussed for
financial inclusion more generally in Focus Box 2.2. Another perhaps
speculative observation is that many of the geographically largest countries have low rates of mobile money penetration, perhaps pointing at
the difficulties in maintaining even basic digital infrastructure over large
areas and dispersed populations. Further discussion of potential breaks
and drivers of mobile money penetration is held back until later in this
section. Perhaps the key message of Figure 6.1 is the severe heterogeneity
in the success of mobile money in establishing itself across Africa; world
leaders in this technology such as Kenya border with world laggards such
as Ethiopia. The question remains, however, as to whether this heterogeneity is merely the result of early adopters and will be corrected as these
services roll out wider over time, or whether there are inherent obstacles
that prevent some countries from even getting off the ground with mobile
money despite the fact that successful blueprints for its integration can be
observed in nearby neighbours.

A wider question, which may be of interest regarding mobile money adoption, is the degree to which mobile money accounts may be supplying the latent demand for conventional bank accounts in countries with low levels of formal financial inclusion. In this case, we would expect to observe a *negative correlation* between the level of regular account ownership and the level of mobile money account ownership. Alternatively, if mobile money accounts utilize much the same infrastructure as conventional bank accounts or are perceived as substitutes or compliments for conventional bank accounts by those who already have access to financial services, we would expect to observe a positive correlation. The graph in Figure 6.2 compares the aggregate level of conventional account ownership and mobile money account ownership by developing region in 2017. The regional abbreviations in the graph correspond to those regions named in full in Table 6.1.

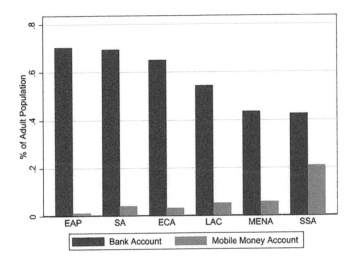

Figure 6.2   2017 levels of conventional and mobile money account ownership by developing region

From Figure 6.2 it can be seen that, at the regional level, there is a negative correlation between the share of individuals with a regular bank account and the share with a mobile money account. Although it would of course be premature to interpret this as a causal explanation for the successful penetration of mobile money into certain regions, it does appear that mobile money has the genuine potential to be especially popular and effective in under-banked regions. What is clear also is that there is no degree to which high conventional account ownership is a precursor to high mobile money account ownership at the regional level; whether it is knowledge, infrastructure, or societal values, there would seem to be no latent *regional* variable driving high conventional account ownership, which is also a necessary condition for high mobile money account ownership. Figure 6.3 presents a scatter plot of the correlation between conventional and mobile money account ownership in 2017, but now between the countries of Sub-Saharan Africa.

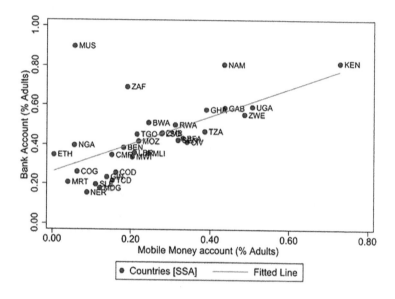

Figure 6.3   2017 correlation of conventional and mobile money account ownership in Sub-Saharan Africa

As can be seen from Figure 6.3, *within* Sub-Saharan Africa there is a strong positive correlation between the penetration of regular bank accounts and that of mobile money, suggesting that, between the countries of Africa, there *are* certain necessary conditions that drive both high conventional account ownership and high mobile money use. Figures 6.4

and 6.5 plot mobile money use[9] in 2017 separately against two candidate variables for latent factors that might be driving both conventional and mobile money account use: (1) GDP per capita in 2017, purchasing power parity adjusted; and (2) fixed broadband subscriptions per 100 people in 2017. The former is a measure of real effective income level, the latter a proxy for the level of digital infrastructure. For the sake of clarity, we omit observation labels on the bunched-together observations. From figures 6.4 and 6.5 it can be seen that there are indeed positive correlations between income level and level of digital infrastructure between the countries of SSA. In summary of these correlations, it would appear that at the regional level mobile money is entering Sub-Saharan Africa more rapidly than all other developing regions *in spite of* the relatively low levels of conventional account ownership, but within SSA there is great disparity between countries in terms of the degree to which mobile money has taken off, and furthermore that there may be necessary preconditions for a widespread adoption of mobile money such as sufficient income and digital infrastructure. Allen et al. (2014) perform regressions of mobile money penetration on a wider set of variables and find that income and GDP growth are the strongest predictors of mobile money use, with other variables such as indices of institutional quality of size of the manufacturing sector entering their regressions insignificantly. Considering the positive impacts of financial inclusion via mobile money, which will shortly be described, more rigorous analysis of the conditions under which African countries widely adopt these services would be of great value to policymakers who wish to encourage their proliferation.

3.2   Impacts of mobile money

Research into the full economic effects of mobile money is still at a nascent stage, and the degree to which impact evaluations into the effects of financial inclusion via other means may be applicable to financial inclusion via mobile money depends crucially on the degree to which these types

---

[9]   The comparatively very wealthy outlier country of Mauritius is dropped from these figures as, when it is included, all other observations are concentrated and low by comparison. Mauritius is also an outlier in that it has a high level of conventional account ownership but a low level of mobile money account ownership, as was seen in Figure 6.3. This suggests that, due to its wealth and also the fact it is an island and geographically distant from the rest of SSA, Mauritius exhibits patterns as if it were a member of a different developing region such as South Asia.

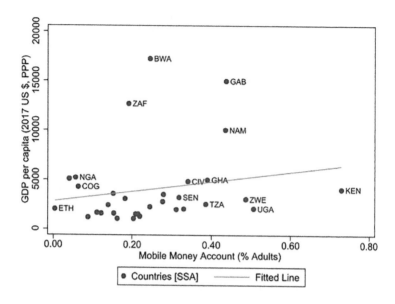

Figure 6.4   2017 correlation of mobile money account ownership
                and income per capita (real, PPP) in Sub-Saharan Africa

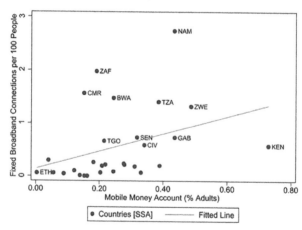

Figure 6.5   2017 correlation of mobile money account ownership
                and fixed broadband subscriptions per capita in
                Sub-Saharan Africa

of financial inclusion are similar. Whilst mobile money providers offer many of the same basic products and services as microfinance banks, the terms and conditions are very different, as may be the manner in which people make use of these products. It would therefore be inappropriate to suggest that increases in use of savings or credit facilities brought about by mobile money may necessarily be expected to have the same impacts as those found for microfinance products. A context-specific study in one region of Ghana showed that mobile money users were more likely to save and invest higher amounts than those who do not use mobile money, including investments in microbusinesses (Apiors & Suzuki 2018). Perhaps the most econometrically rigorous and large-scale study into the diffusion and impacts of mobile money is that of Suri & Jack (2016), which provided important evidence on the differential effects of these services, and financial inclusion more generally, on welfare outcomes for women. These impacts were discussed extensively in Chapter 5, where it will be recalled that, whilst the impact was greater in magnitude for female-headed as opposed to male-headed households, a positive causal effect of access to mobile money on household consumption was found to hold generally in Kenya. Furthermore, access to mobile money was shown to causally reduce the incidence rates of extreme poverty in Kenya, with the authors benchmarking the fact that the effect of mobile money at the point of publication (2016) has lifted almost 200,000 households above the extreme poverty line. This shows a very meaningful impact of mobile money in Kenya, which, as was shown in Table 6.1, is very much the regional leader in terms of mobile money penetration. Other countries that have not yet adopted mobile money to the degree of Kenya may therefore hope to experience significant welfare and poverty gains if they can create the conditions necessary for mobile money take-off.[10]

3.3   Mobile money conclusions

On balance, the rapid advent of mobile money could well act as a gamechanger in the battle to close the financial inclusion gap between

---

[10]   Although the degree to which the impacts of mobile money may 'crowd out' those of other financial inclusion interventions; for example, the introduction of mobile money into a country with a well-developed microfinance market may cause people to switch from utilizing microfinance services and therefore reduce the impacts of this kind of financial inclusion, mitigating the direct observed impacts of mobile money.

Sub-Saharan Africa and the rest of the developing world, with concomitant positive impacts that, at this early empirical stage, appear to be perhaps larger than the impacts of financial inclusion interventions by other means. Some may see mobile banking as an inferior substitute for traditional banking, but it could also be argued that much of traditional banking is outdated in the digital age, and that, by embracing mobile banking more rapidly than other developing regions, Sub-Saharan Africans are actually ahead of the curve. It remains to be seen whether there is a natural boundary on the scope of mobile banking, but the fact that adoption of technologically driven mobile money services expanded so rapidly in many countries, whilst take-up rates of international donor driven microfinance programs was very low across a variety of contexts, is food for thought for researchers and policymakers. This does not necessarily mean that such programs should be abandoned, but certainly that they may be able to learn from mobile money providers. Perhaps by integrating microfinance with mobile money, or scaling down products and services to match the simplicity of the mobile money offerings, there may be scope to address the issue of low take-up rates. Interestingly, Somville & Vandewalle (2018) argue that mobile money networks, with extended banking services, enable to pay public transfers (cash transfers) directly into the recipient's account. They show with a field experiment in India that paying into accounts – and not in cash – substantially increases savings, even in the longer run. The account-based payments, which may be induced by mobile money networks, may have important impacts on the recipient's finances and welfare.

There is clearly a wide disparity between the degree of mobile money penetration *within* Sub-Saharan Africa, and it appears that those countries with the highest rates of exclusion from the conventional banking system are also having difficulty including people via mobile money. This suggests that, whilst mobile money could be a valuable contributor to the fight against financial exclusion, there are certain barriers to the adoption of mobile money in many of the poorest countries. Whether, therefore, adding mobile money to the 'financial inclusion mix' is something that is viable only for countries once they pass a certain threshold, or whether it would be possible to actively put in place the necessary conditions for mobile money adoption in any country, is a question that remains to be answered. But either as a tool to boost financial inclusion in the still largely unbanked SSA countries, or as a complement to other FI interventions in the countries that lead SSA but still lag behind other developing regions in terms of financial inclusion, there is clearly a valuable role that mobile money can play once its potential and limitations become more clearly defined.

4. Fintech at the frontier: blockchain and beyond

Moving beyond mobile money into even more novel and rapidly changing FinTech brings us right to the frontier of what may be happening, and is still to happen, in developing country financial markets. This section must therefore by necessity be more speculative than those that precede it. Hinson et al. (2019) discuss some other aspects of FinTech that relate to agribusinesses and the agricultural sector, demonstrating how specific financial markets can be made more efficient by introduction of specific FinTech developments.[11] However, more generally and as alluded to in the introduction, it is perhaps cryptocurrencies and their partner technology – blockchain – that represent the most obvious next wave of financial innovation that is starting to wash up on the shores of developing countries. Blockchain is the technology that facilitates *crypto-currency transactions*, and acts as a public ledger in which all committed transactions are stored in chronological order and in clear public view (Zheng et al. 2018). However, whilst the transactions themselves are clear and verifiable, the technology is such that the *market participants* themselves are anonymous, and are instead identifiable only as digital keys. In order to avoid central authority, transactions are verified and authorized on the basis of community consensus by other blockchain participants. Once authorized, the 'ledger' – that is, the updated transaction record – is duplicated and distributed across the entire network of computer systems of those involved in the blockchain, therefore rendering it very difficult for these records to be subsequently hidden or altered.

It is the combination of public transparency of transactions and private anonymity of participants that causes blockchain advocates to claim that this transfer system is uniquely resistant to corruption, fraud, and

---

[11] For example, specialized apps and other digital platforms can be designed to facilitate agricultural crop insurance markets or group rental or purchase of agricultural equipment. Hinson et al. (2019) give the specific example of *Hello Tractor*, an app that allows smallholder farmers to easily locate others with whom to collectively rent or buy farm machinery, and facilitates these transactions.

expropriation (Kshetri & Voas 2018). Furthermore, it is argued that, as developing countries are especially vulnerable to these institutional failures, the potential for blockchain to impact economies positively may be greater there than in the developed world. Kshetri & Voas argue that, if government spending and/or contracting were conducted via blockchain, or developing country property transfers took place via this technology, or if taxes and fines could be paid utilizing blockchains, much of the murkiness and leakage around such transactions could be avoided, without the cost of having to expose and infringe upon the privacy of the exact transactors. Other authors, however, have raised concerns about the potential for blockchain to *increase* corruption by facilitating money laundering and tax evasion (Houben & Snyers 2018; Albrecht et al. 2019).

How blockchain and the cryptocurrencies might be expected to interact with financial inclusion is perhaps a little less clear. The anecdotal example of El Salvador presented in the introduction shows that cryptocurrencies can be popular in developing countries if they come in the form of a transfer, but it remains to be seen whether this high early adoption rate will maintain longevity, and whether it was in fact the cryptocurrency that encouraged people to join the digital financial system, or just a sizeable digital transfer in any form. One large advantage of blockchain in fostering financial inclusion may be its relatively low transaction costs, particularly for international transactions. Remittances from abroad are a large share of the GDP of many developing countries, and are especially costly for unbanked individuals due to the need to use cash transfer services – it has therefore been suggested that blockchain technology could facilitate cheaper remittances, and could provide a large incentive to the voluntarily unbanked to open digital accounts so as to benefit from these lower transaction costs (Rühmann et al. 2020). Similarly, direct digital distribution via blockchain could allow international aid providers to disperse funds at a much more disaggregated level, without the need for as many intermediaries, or to monitor intermediaries more precisely via the public digital ledger. Again, this would potentially stimulate financial inclusion if digital wallets were needed to receive these funds, and if the international donors also provided support and guidance to help people set up these digital wallets.

There are, of course, serious concerns over whether these new technologies are fit for the above-described purposes in their current form. Not only are cryptocurrencies and blockchain complex both conceptually and in terms of the infrastructure they require,[12] many of the most famous cryptocurrencies currently suffer from massive price volatility, which would more than outweigh any gains in terms of reduced transaction costs (Caporale & Zekokh 2019). Under the current circumstances, financial inclusion via cryptocurrency wallets and blockchain could end up being more burdensome than emancipating in terms of impact. Nevertheless, the cryptocurrencies themselves and the technology used to transfer them – blockchain – are distinct and different entities, and there is no reason why the latter could not be utilized to transfer money or assets that are more stable, comprehensible, or easily convertible than the former. It may appear that the penetration of such technologies is currently negligible in the developing world, but one would have said the same thing about mobile money just a decade ago. Exploring the theoretical and empirical potential for these technologies to facilitate financial inclusion, and the impacts thereof, may rapidly become a key demand on researchers at the frontier of this field.

5. The future of financial inclusion

This book has taken a tour through the key stages in the evolution of the field of financial inclusion, as well as acquainting the reader with most of the key theories, findings, and established consensuses. Yet there is little in this field that is completely settled or outmoded. Recent data advances, especially as a result of the ever-expanding Findex surveys, provide new opportunities to revisit old questions and concepts, and to continue to track the heterogeneous progress of financial inclusion into the third decade of the new millennium. At the time of publication of this book, the latest round of Findex surveying was delayed due to the global Covid-19 pandemic – it will therefore be of paramount interest to discover what impacts this pandemic and the accompanying lockdowns and recessions

---

[12] As the case of El Salvador demonstrates, to make cryptocurrency viable at the national level requires much more than merely people downloading digital wallets. Cryptocurrency ATMs, point-of-sale terminals, mandates to accept digital currency in private enterprises, plus the ability to send and receive governments payments, are all part of the bitcoin rollout in El Salvador, and it remains to be seen whether these will function efficiently (Zagorsky 2021).

have had on financial inclusion. On the one hand, it might be expected that the lockdown policies of many governments may have rapidly accelerated the transition to digital financial markets, with accompanying rises in financial inclusion, as individuals shied away from cash and physical transactions and became more dependent on government transfers. On the other hand, the economic impacts of these restrictions may have caused a decrease in assets and resources generally, and subsequently less incentive to store money or ability to borrow. Especially concerning is the potential for disproportionately negative consequences on the financial inclusion of women and girls, as well as minority groups who find themselves more tenuously connected to financial systems than the majority, and more prone to financial disenfranchisement in the aftermath of major crises.

Going forward, there is still much work to be done in developing new approaches to continue raising the levels of financial inclusion in many parts of the developing world, and most of all to reduce the stubbornly persistent 'Sub-Saharan Africa gap' and 'gender gap' in financial inclusion. Fortunately, there is growing global awareness and support for these goals, and an ever-increasing research and policy focus. Queen Máxima of the Netherlands, the UN Secretary-General's Special Advocate for Inclusive Finance for Development, said at a recent event that "strong SMEs [small and medium-sized enterprises] are essential for inclusive, equitable and sustainable growth ... [but] SMEs need a range of financial services ... to get there, we need to improve the whole finance ecosystem" (Máxima 2021). Queen Máxima's role as a global advocate for financial inclusion, especially as relates to gender, for both the UN and the G20 is an example of the trend of many leading voices in the international development sphere shifting from seeing FI as one of many side-issues in development to a key central pillar of the global campaign against poverty and disempowerment.

As always, attempts to raise the *levels* of financial inclusion, especially in terms of use in contexts where many FI interventions have suffered from low take-up rates, should be accompanied by rigorous evaluations of the *impacts* of the financial inclusion increases that these interventions hopefully spark, including impacts on an expanded set of outcomes beyond merely economic variables but also societal variables such as measures of (women) empowerment, social engagement, and levels of trust and corruption. In order to fully understand the impacts of financial inclusion, in addition to allowing financial inclusion interventions, programs, and policies to be more generalizable, the focus on the *mechanisms* by which these interventions, programs, and policies lead to broader engagement with the financial system and in turn to lower- and higher-order outcomes must take a key role in the next generation of theoretical and empirical research. Many of the excellent papers discussed in this book have already begun taking steps in this direction.

The field of financial inclusion is a very exciting one both for practical and intellectual reasons. As a relatively new field, with relatively recent but rapidly expanding quality data sources, there is much scope for a wider set of development researchers to join the academic conversation. This is a conversation that may often begin in the halls of universities and the pages of academic journals but, as has been seen with numerous examples throughout this book, can rapidly transfer to the real-world settings of field experiments and larger-scale rollouts of programs by international development organizations, developing country governments, and private banks. The results of quality academic research can have fast and tangible impacts on the real world of developing countries, and on the lives of people that live there. It is equally important that, in a world with large levels of poverty and disenfranchisement and limited resources with which to attempt to alleviate them, failing programs and interventions are quickly identified and stopped or adapted, such that resources are not wasted that could be used to help others elsewhere. Perhaps most exciting of all, the study of financial inclusion takes us right to the frontier of technology and innovation, as well as of theory and econometric identification. The rise of mobile money and other even newer FinTech presents ever-expanding opportunities both to tackle financial exclusion through international interventions, or even for people to include themselves in the financial system without help from external parties. This is happening in real time, and in order to keep pace with the changes and evolution of developing country financial systems and their product and service offerings, researchers must act fast to harness and evaluate the impacts of these changes. This is a challenge, but a very exciting challenge. We sincerely hope this book has been more than merely a reference work for existing financial inclusion scholars and policymakers, but has also acted as an inspiration for new and diverse talent to join the field.

References

Abor, C.J.Y., C.K.D. Adjasi, & R. Lensink (eds) (2020). *Contemporary Issues in Development Finance*, Routledge, London.

Abor, C.J.Y., C.K.D. Adjasi, & R. Lensink (2021). Introduction to *Contemporary Issues in Development Finance*, in C.J.Y. Abor, C.K.D. Adjasi, & R. Lensink (eds), *Contemporary Issues in Development Finance*, Routledge, London, 1–19.

Acemoglu, D., S. Johnson, & J.A. Robinson (2001). The colonial origins of comparative development: An empirical investigation. *American Economic Review*, 91(5), 1369–1401.

Adoho, F., S. Chakravarty, D.T. Korkoyah, M. Lundberg, & A. Tasneem (2014). The impact of an adolescent girls employment program: The EPAG project in Liberia. Policy Research working paper, no. WPS 6832, Impact Evaluation series, no. IE 121. World Bank Group, Washington, DC. Retrieved from http://documents.worldbank.org/curated/en/610391468299085610/Theimpact-of-an-adolescent-girls-employment-program-the-EPAG-project-in-Liberia

Agarwal, S., T. Kigabo, C. Minoiu, A.F. Presbitero, & A.F. Silva (2021). Serving the Underserved: Microcredit as a Pathway to Commercial Banks. *Finance and Economics Discussion Series* 2021-041. Washington, DC: Board of Governors of the Federal Reserve System, https://doi.org/10.17016/FEDS.2021.041. Forthcoming in *Review of Economics and Statistics*.

Aggarwal, S., & L. Klapper (2013). Designing government policies to expand financial inclusion: Evidence from around the world. *Journal of Finance*, 56(3), 1029–1051.

Ahmed S.M. (2005). Intimate partner violence against women: Experiences from a woman-focused development programme in Matlab, Bangladesh. *Journal of Health, Population, and Nutrition*, 23(1), 95–101.

Akerlof, G. (1976). The economics of caste and of the rat race and other woeful tales. *The Quarterly Journal of Economics*, 90(4), 599–617.

Albrecht, C., K. Duffin, S. Hawkins, & V. Morales Rocha (2019). The use of cryptocurrencies in the money laundering process. *Journal of Money Laundering Control*, 22(2), 210–216.

Alkire, S., M. Meinzen-Dick, A. Peterman, A. Quisumbing, G. Seymour, & A. Vaz (2013). The women's empowerment in agriculture index. *World Development*, 52, 71–91.

Allen, F., E. Carletti, R. Cull, J. Qian, L. Senbet, & P. Valenzuela (2014). The African financial development and financial inclusion gaps. *Journal of African Economies*, 23(5), 614–642.

Allen, F., E. Carletti, R. Cull, J. Qian, L. Senbet, & P. Valenzuela (2021). Improving access to banking: Evidence from Kenya. *Review of Finance*, 25(2), 403–447.

Allen, F., A. Demirgüç-Kunt, L. Klapper, M. Soledad, & M. Peria (2016). The foundations of financial inclusion: Understanding ownership and use of formal accounts. *Journal of Financial Intermediation*, 27, 1–30.

Amoah, L., C.K.D. Adjasi, I. Soumare, K.A. Osie, C.J.Y. Abor, E.B. Anarfo, C. Amo-Yartey, & I. Otchere (2020), Finance, Economic Growth, and Development, in C.J.Y. Abor, C.K.D. Adjasi, & R. Lensink (eds), *Contemporary Issues in Development Finance*, Routledge, London, Chapter 2, 20–51.

Anderberg, D., & H. Rainer (2011). Domestic Abuse: Instrumental Violence and Economics Incentives. *CESifo Working Paper Series* 3673, CESifo Group, Munich.

Anderson, S., & J. Baland (2002). The economics of Roscas and intrahousehold resource allocation. *Quarterly Journal of Economics*, 117(3), 963–995.

Andrianaivo, M., & Kpodar, K. (2011). ICT, Financial Inclusion, and Growth: Evidence from African Countries. IMF Working Papers, 11(73), Washington, DC.

Angelucci, M., D. Karlan, & J. Zinman (2015). Microcredit impacts: Evidence from a randomized microcredit program placement experiment by Compartamos Banco. *American Economic Journal: Applied Economics*, 7(1), 151–182.

Anjini, K., C. Nagabhushana, R. Sarkar, R. Shah, & G. Singh (2021). *The Policies that Empower Women: Empirical Evidence from India's National Rural Livelihoods Project*, 3ie, Working Paper 40.

Ansar, S., R. Deshpande, L. Klapper, & A. Koning (2021). What Drives the Financial Inclusion Gender Gap for Young Women? [Blog]. Retrieved from https://www.cgap.org/blog/what-drives-financial-inclusion-gender-gap -young-women

Apiors, E., & A. Suzuki. (2018). Mobile money, individuals' payments, remittances, and investments: Evidence from the Ashanti Region, Ghana. *Sustainability*, 10(5), 1–26.

Armendáriz, B., & J. Morduch (2010). *The Economics of Microfinance* (2nd edn), MIT, London.

Arner, D., J. Barberis, & R. Buckley (2015). The Evolution of Fintech: A New Post-Crisis Paradigm. *The University of New South Wales (UNSW) and the University of Hong Kong, UNSW Law Research Paper*, No. 2016-62, Hong Kong, Sydney.

Aron, J. (2018). Mobile money and the economy: A review of the evidence. *The World Bank Research Observer*, 33(2), 135–188.

Arun, T., & R. Kamath (2015). Financial inclusion: Policies and practices. *IIMB Management Review*, 27(4), 267–287.

Ashraf, N., D. Karlan, & W. Yin (2010). Female empowerment: Impact of a commitment savings product in the Philippines. *World Development*, 38(3), 333–344.

Attanasio, O., B. Augsburg, R. De Haas, E. Fitzsimons, & H. Harmgart (2015). The impacts of microfinance: Evidence from joint-liability lending in Mongolia. *American Economic Journal: Applied Economics*, 7(1), 90–122.

Augsburg, B., R. De Haas, H. Harmgart, & C. Meghir (2015). The impacts of microcredit: Evidence from Bosnia and Herzegovina. *American Economic Journal: Applied Economics*, 7(1), 183–203.

Banerjee, A., E. Duflo, R. Glennerster, & C. Kinnan (2015a). The miracle of microfinance? Evidence from a randomized evaluation. *American Economic Journal: Applied Economics*, 7(1), 22–53.

Banerjee, A., E. Duflo, N. Goldberg, D. Karlan, R. Osei, W. Pariente, J. Shapiro, B. Thuysbaert, & C. Udry (2015b). A multifaceted program causes lasting progress for the very poor: Evidence from six countries. *Science*, 348(6236), 1260799–1260799.

Banerjee, R., R. Donato, & A.A. Maruta (2020). The Effects of Financial Inclusion on Development Outcomes: New Insights from ASEAN and East Asian Countries. ERIA Discussion Paper Series, no. 342: ERIA-DP-2020-15.

Banerjee, A., E. Duflo, & G. Sharma (2021). Long-Term Effects of the Targeting the Ultra Poor Program. SSRN Electronic Journal.

Basargekar, P. (2009). Microcredit and a macro leap: An impact analysis of Annapurna Mahila Mandal (AMM), an urban microfinance institution in India. *IUP Journal of Financial Economics*, 7(3/4), 105–120.

Bauchet, J., C. Marshall, L. Starita, J. Thomas, & A. Yalouris (2011). Latest Findings from Randomized Evaluations of Microfinance. *Access to Finance Forum Reports* by CGAP and Its Partners, No. 2, December.

Beaman, L., E. Duflo, R. Pande, & P. Topalova (2012). Female leadership raises aspirations and educational attainment for girls: A policy experiment in India. *Science*, 335(6068), 582–586.

Beck, T. (2014). Finance, growth, and stability: Lessons from the crisis. *Journal of Financial Stability*, 10(1), 1–6.

Beck, T., & R. Levine (2002). Industry growth and capital accumulation: Does having a market- or bank-based system matter? *Journal of Financial Economics*, 64, 147–180.

Beck, T., & R. Levine (2004). Stock markets, banks and growth: Panel evidence. *Journal of Banking and Finance*, 28, 423–442.

Beck, T., A. Demirgüç-Kunt, & R. Levine (1999). A New Database on Financial Development and Structure. *Financial Sector Discussion Paper* No. 2, The World Bank.

Beck, T., A. Demirgüç-Kunt, & R. Levine (2003a), Law and finance: Why does legal origin matter? *Journal of Comparative Economics*, 31, 653–675.

Beck, T., A. Demirgüç-Kunt, & R. Levine (2003b). Law, endowments, and finance. *Journal of Financial Economics*, 70, 137–181.

Beck, T., A. Demirgüç-Kunt, M. Soledad, & M. Peria (2007). Reaching out: Access to and use of banking services across countries. *Journal of Financial Economics*, 85, 234–266.

Belissa, T.K., E. Bulte, F. Cecchi, S. Gangopadhyay, & R. Lensink (2019). Liquidity constraints, informal institutions, and the adoption of weather insurance: A randomized controlled trial in Ethiopia. *Journal of Development Economics*, 140, 269–278.

Belissa, T.K., E. Bulte, F. Cecchi, S. Gangopadhyay, & R. Lensink (2020). Improving trust and relaxing liquidity constraints to enhance uptake of weather insurance in Ethiopia, *Formative Evaluation Report*, International

Initiative for Impact Evaluation (3ie). Retrieved from https://3ieimpact.org/evidence-hub/publications/other-evaluations/improving-trust-and-relaxing-liquidity-constraints

Belissa, T.K., R. Lensink, & A. Marr (2021). *Uptake and Impact of Interlinked Index-based Insurance with Credit and Inputs.* Unpublished manuscript, Groningen.

Benhassine, N., F. Devoto, E. Duflo, P. Dupas, & V. Pouliquen (2015). Turning a shove into a nudge? A 'labeled cash transfer' for education. *American Economic Journal: Economic Policy*, 7(3), 86–125.

Berge, L.I.O, K. Bjorvatn, & B. Tungodden (2015). Human and financial capital for microenterprise development: Evidence from a field experiment. *Tanzania Management Science*, 61(4), 707–722. https://doi.org/10.1287/mnsc.2014.1933

Bernard, T., S. Dercon, K. Orkin, & A.S. Taffesse (2015). Will video kill the radio star? Assessing the potential of targeted exposure to role models through video. *World Bank Economic Review*, 29(1), 226–237.

Bernard, T., S. Dercon, K. Orkin, & A.S. Taffesse (2019). Parental aspirations for children's education: Is there a 'girl effect'? Experimental evidence from rural Ethiopia. *AEA Papers and Proceedings*, 109, 107–132.

Besley, T., K. Burchardi, & M. Ghatak (2021). The Role of Finance in the Process of Development: Improving Access versus Reducing Frictions. Retrieved from https://personal.lse.ac.uk/ghatak/FinFric.pdf

Blair, G., & K. Imai (2012). Statistical analysis of list experiments. *Political Analysis*, 20(1), 47–77.

Bloch, F., & V. Rao (2002). Terror as a bargaining instrument: A case study of dowry violence in rural India. *American Economic Review*, 92, 1029–1042.

Blumberg, R. (1989). Entrepreneurship, Credit, and Gender in the Informal Sector of the Dominican Republic, in *Women in Development: A.I.D.'s Experience, 1973–1985*, Vol. 2, USAID, Center for Development Information and Evaluation, Washington, DC.

Bossuroy, T., M. Goldstein, D. Karlan, H. Kazianga, W. Pariente, P. Premand, C. Thomas, C. Udry, J. Vaillan, & K. Wright (2021). Pathways out of Extreme Poverty: Tackling Psychosocial and Capital Constraints with a Multi-faceted Social Protection Program in Niger. *Policy Research Working Paper* 9562, The World Bank.

Breza, E., & C. Kinnan (2021). Measuring the equilibrium impacts of credit: Evidence from the Indian microfinance crisis. *Quarterly Journal of Economics*, 136(3), 1447–1497.

Bruhn, M., & I. Love (2014). The real impact of improved access to finance: Evidence from Mexico. *Journal of Finance*, 69(3), 1347–1376.

Bulte, E., & R. Lensink (2019). Women's empowerment and domestic abuse: Experimental evidence from Vietnam. *European Economic Review*, 115, 172–191.

Bulte, E., & R. Lensink (2020). *Women's Empowerment and Domestic Abuse.* Faculty of Economics & Business, University of Groningen. Unpublished research memorandum.

Bulte, E., F. Cecchi, R. Lensink, A. Marr, & M. van Asseldonk (2020). Do crop insurance-certified seed bundles crowd-in investments? Experimental evidence from Kenya. *Journal of Economic Behavior and Organization*, 180, 744–757.

Bulte, E., R. Lensink, & N. Vu (2017). Do gender and business trainings affect business outcomes? Experimental evidence from Vietnam. *Management Science*, 63(9), 2885–2902.

Burgess, R., & R. Pande (2005). Do rural banks matter? Evidence from the Indian social banking experiment. *American Economic Review*, 95(3), 780–795.

Cai, H., Y. Chen, H. Fang, & L. Zhou (2015). The effect of microinsurance on economic activities: Evidence from a randomized field experiment. *Review of Economics and Statistics*, 97(2), 287–300.

Caporale, G., & T. Zekokh (2019). Modelling volatility of cryptocurrencies using Markov-switching GARCH models. *Research in International Business and Finance*, 48, 143–155.

Casaburi, L., & J. Willis (2018). Time versus state in insurance: Experimental evidence from contract farming in Kenya. *American Economic Review*, 108(12), 3778–3813.

Cecchi, F., A. Garcia, R. Lensink, & B. Wydick (2021). *Aspirational Hope, Dairy Farming Practices, and Milk Production: Evidence from a Randomized Controlled Trial in Bolivia*. Unpublished manuscript, Faculty of Economics and Business, University of Groningen.

Chamie, J. (2016). 320 million children in single parent families. Inter Press Service. October 15. Retrieved from www.globalissues.org

Chemin, M. (2008). The benefits and costs of microfinance: Evidence from Bangladesh. *Journal of Development Studies*, 44, 463–484.

Chibba, M. (2009). Financial inclusion, poverty reduction and the millennium development goals. *European Journal of Development Research*, 21(2), 213–230.

Chima, M.M., A.A. Babajide, A. Adegboye, S. Kehinde, & O. Fasheyitan (2021). The relevance of financial inclusion on sustainable economic growth in Sub-Saharan African nations. *Sustainability*, 13, 5581. http://doi.org/10.3390/su13105581.

Chliova, M., J. Brinckmann, & N. Rosenbusch (2015). Is microcredit a blessing for the poor? A meta-analysis examining development outcomes and contextual considerations. *Journal of Business Venturing*, 30(3), 467–487.

Collins, D., Jonathan, M., Stuart, R. & O. Ruthven (2009). *Portfolios of the Poor: How the World's Poor Live on $2 a Day*. Princeton University Press, Princeton, New Jersey.

Crépon, B., F. Devoto, E. Duflo, & W. Parienté (2015). Estimating the impact of microcredit on those who take it up: Evidence from a randomized experiment in Morocco. *American Economic Journal: Applied Economics*, 7(1), 123–150.

Dabla-Norris, E., Y. Ji, R.M. Townsend, & D.F. Unsal (2021). Distinguishing constraints on financial inclusion and their impact on GDP, TFP, and the distribution of income. *Journal of Monetary Economics*, 117, 1–18.

Dahal, M., & N. Fiala (2020). What do we know about the impact of microfinance? The problems of statistical power and precision. *World Development*, 128, 104773.

Dasgupta, N., M. Scircle, & M. Hunsinger (2015). Female Peers in Small Work Groups Enhance Women's Motivation, Verbal Participation, and Career Aspirations in Engineering. *Proceedings of the National Academy of Sciences*.

De Mel, S., D. McKenzie, & C. Woodruff (2008). Returns to capital in microenterprises: Evidence from a field experiment. *Quarterly Journal of Economics*, 123(4), 1329–1372.

De Mel, S., D. McKenzie, & C. Woodruff (2009). Are women more credit constrained? Experimental evidence on gender and microenterprise returns. *American Economic Journal: Applied Economics*, 1(3), 1–32.

Deaton, A. (1991), Saving and liquidity constraints. *Econometrica*, 59(5), 1221–1248.

Deaton, A., & N. Cartwright (2018). Understanding and misunderstanding randomized controlled trials. *Social Science & Medicine*, 210, 2–21.

Demirgüç-Kunt, A., & R. Levine (2001), *Financial Structures and Economic Growth: A Cross-Country Comparison of Banks, Markets and Development*, MIT Press, Cambridge, MA.

Demirgüç-Kunt, A., & L. Klapper (2013). Measuring financial inclusion: The global Findex database. *Brookings Papers on Economic Activity*, Spring, 279–321.

Demirgüç-Kunt, A., L. Klapper, D. Singer, S. Ansar, & J. Hess (2017). *The Global Findex Database: Measuring Financial Inclusion and the Fintech Revolution*. World Bank Presentation.

Demirgüç-Kunt, A., L. Klapper, D. Singer, S. Ansar, & J. Hess (2018). *The Global Findex Database 2017: Measuring Financial Inclusion and the FinTech Revolution*, World Bank, Washington, DC.

D'Espallier, B., I. Guérin, & R. Mersland (2011). Women and repayment in microfinance: A global analysis. *World Development*, 39(5), 758–772.

Dichter T., & M. Harper (2007). *What's Wrong with Microfinance?* Practical Action Publishing, Rugby.

Duflo, E. (2003). Grandmothers and granddaughters: Old-age pensions and intrahousehold allocation in South Africa. *World Bank Economic Review*, 17, 1–25.

Duflo, E. (2012). Women empowerment and economic development. *Journal of Economic Literature*, 50(4), 1051–1079.

Duflo, E. (2013). *Hope, Aspirations and the Design of the Fight Against Poverty*. Stanford University Center for Ethics in Society, Stanford, CA.

Duflo, E., & C. Udry (2004). Intra Household Resource Allocation in Cote d'Ivoire: Social Norms, Separate Accounts and Consumption Choices. *NBER Working Paper*, No. 10498.

Dunford, C. (2003). The Holy Grail of Microfinance: Helping the poor and sustainable: Microfinance evolution, achievements and challenges. In *Microfinance: Evolution, Achievement and Challenges*, ITDG, London, 150–154.

Dupas, P., & J. Robinson (2013a). Savings constraints and microenterprise development: Evidence from a field experiment in Kenya. *American Economic Journal: Applied Economics*, 5(1), 163–192.

Dupas, P., & J. Robinson (2013b). Why don't the poor save more? Evidence from health savings experiments. *American Economic Review*, 103(4), 1138–1171.

Duvendack, M., & P. Mader (2020). Impact of financial inclusion in low- and middle-income countries: A systematic review of reviews. *Journal of Economic Surveys*, 34(3), 594–629.

Duvendack, M., R. Palmer-Jones, J.G. Copestake, L. Hooper, Y. Loke, & N. Rao (2011). *What is the Evidence of the Impact of Microfinance on the Well-Being of*

Poor People? EPPI-Centre, Social Science Research Unit, Institute of Education, University of London.

Ellerman, D. (2007). Microfinance: Some Conceptual and Methodological Problems, in T. Dichter & M. Harper (eds), *What's Wrong with Microfinance?* Practical Action Publishing, Rugby, 149–161.

Eswaran, M., & N. Malhotra (2011). Domestic violence and women's autonomy in developing countries: Theory and evidence. *Canadian Journal of Economics*, 44, 1222–1263.

Farmer, A., & J. Tiefenthaler (1997). An economic analysis of domestic violence. *Review of Social Economy*, 55(3), 337–358.

Field, E., S. Jayachandran, R. Pande, & N. Rigol (2016). Friendship at work: Can peer effects catalyze female entrepreneurship. *American Economic Journal: Economic Policy*, 8(2), 125–153.

Fisher, I. (1930). *The Theory of Interest*. Macmillan, New York.

Gabor, D., & S. Brooks (2017). The digital revolution in financial inclusion: International development in the Fintech era. *New Political Economy*, 22(4), 423–436.

Garcia, A., & R. Lensink (2019). Microfinance-Plus: A Review and Avenues for Research, in M. Hudon, M. Labie, & A. Sfaraz (eds), *Research Agenda for Financial Inclusion and Microfinance*, Edward Elgar Publishing, Cheltenham, UK, and Northampton, MA, USA, Chapter 9, 111–125.

Garcia, A., R. Lensink, & M. Voors (2020). Does microcredit increase aspirational hope? Evidence from a group lending scheme in Sierra Leone. *World Development*, 128, 104861. https://doi.org/10.1016/j.worlddev.2019.104861

Garikipati, S. (2008). The impact of lending to women on household vulnerability and women's empowerment: Evidence from India. *World Development*, 36(12), 2620–2642. https://doi.org/10.1016/j.worlddev.2007.11.008

Genicot, G., & D. Ray (2017). Aspirations and inequality. *Econometrica*, 85(2), 489–519. https://doi.org/10.3982/ecta13865

Ghosh, P., A. Mookherjee, & D. Ray (2001). Credit Rationing in Developing Countries: An Overview of the Theory, in A. Mookherjee & D. Ray (eds), *Readings in the Theory of Economic Development*, Blackwell, London, Chapter 11, 283–302.

Ghosh, S. (2021). How important is trust in driving financial inclusion? *Journal of Behavioral and Experimental Finance*, 30, issue C.

Ghosh, S., & D. Vinod (2017). What constrains financial inclusion for women? Evidence from Indian micro data. *World Development*, 92, 60–81.

Giné, X., & G. Mansuri (2021). Money or management? A field experiment on constraints to entrepreneurship in rural Pakistan. *Economic Development and Cultural Change*, 70(1), 41–86. https://doi.org/10.1086/707502

Glennerster, R., C. Walsh, & L. Diaz-Martin (2019). *A Practical Guide to Measuring Women's and Girls' Empowerment in Impact Evaluations*. J-PAL Poverty Action Lab, MIT.

Goldstein, M., & C. Udry (2008). The profits of power: Land rights and agricultural investment in Ghana. *Journal of Political Economy*, 116(6), 981–1022.

Greenwood, J., & B. Jovanovic (1990). Financial development, growth, and the distribution of income. *Journal of Political Economy*, 98(5, Part 1), 1076–1107.

Guérin, I., S. Kumar, & I. Agier (2010). Microfinance and women's empowerment: Do relationships between women matter? Lessons from rural Southern India. Centre Emile Bernheim Research Institute in Management Sciences working papers CEB10:053. Centre Emile Bernheim, Brussels.

Hannig, A., & S. Jansen (2010). Financial Inclusion and Financial Stability: Current Policy Issues. SSRN *Electronic Journal*.

Hansen, N. (2015) The development of psychological capacity for action: The empowering effect of a microfinance programme on women in Sri Lanka. *Journal of Social Issues*, 71(3), 597–613. http://doi.org/10.1111/josi.12130

Hansen, N., M. Huis, & R. Lensink (2021). Microfinance Services and Women's Empowerment, in S.J. Leire, J.L. Retolaza, & L. Van Liedekerke (eds), *International Handbooks in Business Ethics: Handbook on Ethics in Finance*. Springer, Cham, Switzerland, 161–182.

Hastings, J., & J. Shapiro (2013). Fungibility and consumer choice: Evidence from commodity price shocks. *Quarterly Journal of Economics*, 128(4), 1449–1498.

Hawkins, J., & D. Mihaljek (2001). The Banking Industry in the Emerging Market Economies: Competition, Consolidation and Systemic Stability: An Overview, in Settlements, Bank for International (eds), *The Banking Industry in the Emerging Market Economies: Competition, Consolidation and Systemic Stability*, vol. 04, Bank for International Settlements.

Helms, B. (2006). *Access for All: Building Inclusive Financial Systems*. The World Bank Group.

Hermes, N., & R. Lensink (2007). The empirics of microfinance: What do we know? *Economic Journal*, 117(517), F1–F11.

Hermes, N., & R. Lensink (2021). Microfinance and development, in C.J.Y. Abor, C. Adjasi, & R. Lensink (eds), *Contemporary Issues in Development Finance*, Routledge, London, Chapter 3, 51–73.

Hill, R.V., J. Hoddinott, & D. Kumar (2013). Adoption of weather-index insurance: Learning from willingness to pay among a panel of households in rural Ethiopia. *Agricultural Economics*, 44(4–5), 385–398.

Hill, R.V., N. Kumar, N. Magnan, S. Makhija, F. de Nicola, D.J. Spielman, & P.S. Ward (2019). Ex ante and ex post effects of Hybrid Index Insurance in Bangladesh. *Journal of Development Economics*, 136, 1–17.

Hinson, R., R. Lensink, & A. Mueller (2019). Transforming agribusiness in developing countries: SDGs and the role of FinTech. *Current Opinion in Environmental Sustainability*, 41, 1–9.

Holtz-Eakin, D., D. Joulfaian, & H. Rosen (1994). Entrepreneurial decisions and liquidity restraints. *Rand Journal of Economics*, 25(2), 334–347.

Honohan, P. (2004). Financial development, growth, and poverty: How close are the links? *Policy Research Working Paper*, No. 3203, World Bank, Washington, DC.

Honohan, P. (2008). Cross-country variation in household access to financial services. *Journal of Banking and Finance*, 32, 2493–2500.

Houben, R., & A. Snyers (2018). Cryptocurrencies and blockchain: Legal context and implications for financial crime, money laundering and tax evasion. European Parliament, Brussels.

Hudon, M., & J. Sandberg, J. (2013). The ethical crisis in microfinance: Issues, findings, and implications. *Business Ethics Quarterly*, 23(4), 561–589.

Hudon, M., M. Labie, & A. Szafarz (2019). *A Research Agenda for Financial Inclusion and Microfinance* (1st edn). Edward Elgar Publishing, Cheltenham, UK and Northampton, MA, USA.

Hughes, C. (Host) (2021). Economics 102 with Prof Abhijit Banerjee (No. 31) [Audio podcast episode], in *Conversations with Coleman*, https://colemanhughes.org/

Huis, M., N. Hansen, R. Lensink, & S. Otten (2017). A three-dimensional model of women's empowerment: Implications in the field of microfinance and future directions. *Frontiers in Psychology*, 28 September, https://doi.org/10.3389/fpsyg.2017.01678.

Huis, M., N. Hansen, R. Lensink, & S. Otten (2020). A relational perspective on women's empowerment: Intimate partner violence and empowerment among women entrepreneurs in Vietnam. *British Journal of Social Psychology*, 59(2), 365–386. https://doi.org/10.1111/bjso.12348

Hussmans R. (2005). Measuring the informal economy: From employment in the informal sector to informal employment. Policy Integration Department Bureau of Statistics International Labour Office Working Paper No. 53 Geneva.

Iacovone, L., F. Rauch, & L. Winters (2013). Trade as an engine of creative destruction: Mexican experience with Chinese competition. *Journal of International Economics*, 89(2), 379–392.

ILO (2014). *Profits and Poverty: The Economics of Forced Labour*. ILO, Geneva, Switzerland.

IMF (2020). *Measuring Financial Access: 10 Years of the IMF Financial Access Survey*. ISBN 9781513538853.

Inman, R.P. (2009). Flypaper Effect. In *The New Palgrave Dictionary of Economics*. Palgrave Macmillan, London.

Jeong, H., & R.M. Townsend (2007). Sources of TFP growth: Occupational choice and financial deepening. *Economic Theory*, 32(1), 179–221.

Jerven, M., Y. Kale, M. Duncan, & M. Nyoni (2015). GDP revisions and updating statistical systems in Sub-Saharan Africa: Reports from the statistical offices in Nigeria, Liberia and Zimbabwe. *Journal of Development Studies*, 51(2), 194–207.

Kabeer, N. (1999). Resources, agency, achievements: Reflections on the measurement of women's empowerment. *Development and Change*, 30(3), 435–464.

Karlan, D., R. Osei, I. Osei-Akoto, & C. Udry (2014). Agricultural decisions after relaxing credit and risk constraints. *Quarterly Journal of Economics*, 129, 597–652.

Karlan, D., B. Savonitto, B. Thuysbaert, & C. Udry (2017). Impact of savings groups on the lives of the poor. *Proceedings of The National Academy of Sciences*, 114(12), 3079–3084.

Kato, M.P., & J. Kratzer (2013). Empowering women through microfinance: Evidence from Tanzania. *ACRN Journal of Entrepreneurship Perspectives*, 2(1), 31–59.

Khan, S., & Arefin, H. (2013). Safety net, social protection, and sustainable poverty reduction: A review of the evidences and arguments for developing countries. *IOSR Journal of Humanities and Social Science*, 15(2), 23–29.

Khawari, A. (2004). Microfinance: Does it hold its promises? A survey of recent literature, *HWWA Discussion Papers* 276, Hamburg Institute of International Economics (HWWA).

King, R.G., & R. Levine (1999). Finance and growth: Schumpeter might be right. *Quarterly Journal of Economics*, 108, 717–737.

Kochar, A., C. Nagabhushana, R. Sarkar, R. Shah, & G. Singh (2022). Financial access and women's role in household decisions: Empirical evidence from India's National Rural Livelihoods project. *Journal of Development Economics*, 155, 102821. https://doi.org/10.1016/j.jdeveco.2022.102821

Koczberski, G. (1998). Women in development: A critical analysis. *Third World Quarterly*, 19(3), 395–410.

Koomson, I., A. Villano Renato, & D. Hadley (2020). Intensifying financial inclusion through the provision of financial literacy training: A gendered perspective. *Applied Economics*, 52(4), 375–387.

Kshetri, N., & J. Voas (2018). Blockchain in developing countries. *IEEE IT Professional*, 20(2), 11–14.

Kulkarni, V.S. (2011). Women's empowerment and microfinance: An Asian perspective study. *International Fund for Agricultural Development*, 13, 11–37.

La Porta, R., F. Lopez-de-Silanes, A. Shleifer, & R.W. Vishny (1998). Law and finance. *Journal of Political Economy*, 106, 1113–1155.

La Porta, R., F. Lopez-de-Silanes, A. Shleifer, & R. Vishny (2000). Investor protection and corporate governance. *Journal of Financial Economics*, 58, 3–27.

Lensink, R., & E. Bulte (2019). Can we Improve the Impact of Microfinance? A Survey of the Recent Literature and Potential Avenues for Success, in A.N. Berger, P. Molyneux, & J.O. Wilson (eds), *Oxford Handbook of Banking*, Oxford University Press, Oxford, Chapter 13, 404–431.

Levine, R. (1998). The legal environment, banks, and long-run economic growth. *Journal of Money, Credit, and Banking*, 30, 596–620.

Leyshon, A., & N. Thrift (1995). Geographies of financial exclusion: Financial abandonment in Britain and the United States. *Transactions of the Institute of British Geographers*, 21, 312–341.

Liu, Y., K. Chen, & R.V. Hill (2020). Delayed premium payment, insurance adoption, and household investment in Rural China. *America Journal of Agricultural Economics*, 102(4), 1117–1197.

Lloyd-Ellis, H., & D. Bernhardt (2000). Enterprise, inequality, and economic development. *Review of Economic Studies*, V(67), 147–168.

Lucas, R. (1988). On the mechanics of economic development. *Journal of Monetary Economics*, 22, 3–42. https://www.parisschoolofeconomics.eu/docs/darcillon-thibault/lucasmechanicseconomicgrowth.pdf

Lybbert, T., & Wydick, B. (2018). Poverty, aspirations, and the economics of hope. *Economic Development and Cultural Change*, 66(4), 709–753. https://doi.org/10.1086/696968

Madestam, A. (2014). Informal finance: A theory of moneylenders. *Journal of Development Economics*, 107, 157–174.

Malapit, H. (2012). Why do spouses hide income? *Journal of Socio-Economics*, 41, 584–593.

Manig, W. (1990). Formal and informal credit markets for agricultural development in developing countries: The example of Pakistan. *Journal of Rural Studies*, 6(2), 209–215.

Mas, I. (2011). Why are banks so scarce in developing countries? A regulatory and infrastructure perspective. *Critical Review*, 23(1–2), 135–145.

Mayoux, L. (1999). Questioning virtuous spirals: Micro-finance and women's empowerment in Africa. *Journal of International Development*, 11(7), 957–984. https://doi.org/10.1002/(sici)1099-1328(199911/12)11:7

McKenzie, D., & C. Woodruff (2013). What are we learning from business training and entrepreneurship evaluations around the developing world? *World Bank Research Observer*, 29(1), 48–82. https://doi.org/10.1093/wbro/lkt007

Meyer, R.L. (2007). Measuring the impact of microfinance. In T. Dichter & M. Harper (eds), *What's Wrong with Microfinance?* Practical Action Publishing, Rugby.

Miguel, E., & M. Kremer (2004). Worms: Identifying impacts on education and health in the presence of treatment externalities. *Econometrica*, 72(1), 159–217.

Mizan, A. (1993). Women's Decision-making Power in Rural Bangladesh: A Study of the Grameen Bank. In Abu Wahid (ed.), *The Grameen Bank: Poverty Relief in Bangladesh*, Westview, Boulder, CO, 97–126.

Mohiuddin, S. (2015). *Private Sector Leadership in Financial Inclusion*. Corporate Citizenship Center, U.S. Chamber of Commerce Foundation.

Navaretti, G.B., G. Calzolari, & A.F. Pozzolo (2017). FinTech and banks: Friends or foes? *European Economy: Banks, Regulation, and the Real Sector*, December.

Nkoa, B.E., & J.S. Song (2020). Does institutional quality affect financial inclusion in Africa? A panel data analysis. *Economic Systems*, 44(4), 1–11. https://doi.org/10.1016/j.ecosys.2020.100836

Nkurunziza, J.D., L. Ndikumana, & P. Nyamoya (2012). The Financial Sector in Burundi. *National Bureau of Economic Research NBER Working Paper* 18289.

North, D.C. (1990). *Institutions, Institutional Change, and Economic Performance*, Cambridge University Press, Cambridge.

Omar, M.A., & K. Inaba (2020). Does financial inclusion reduce poverty and income inequality in developing countries? A panel data analysis. *Journal of Economic Structures*, 9(37), 1–25. https://doi.org/10.1186/s40008-020-00214-4

Ozili, P. (2020). Financial inclusion research around the world: A review. *Forum for Social Economics*, 49(2), 1–23.

Pagano, M. (1993). Financial markets and growth: An overview. *European Economic Review*, 37 (2–3), 613–622.

Pandey, P., S. Sehgal, & W. Ahmad (2020). Banking system integration in South Asia. In S. Sehgal, W. Ahmad, P. Pandey, & S. Saini (2020), *Economic and Financial Integration in South Asia* (1st edn), Routledge, London, 137–146.

Patrick, H. T. (1966). Financial development and economic growth in underdeveloped countries. *Economic Development and Cultural Change*, 14, 174–189.

Pew Research Center (2015). Cell phones in Africa: Communication Lifeline, April 2015 www.pewresearch.org

Philippon, T. (2016). The Fintech opportunity. *National Bureau of Economic Research Working Paper* 22476.

Pitt, M.M., & S.R. Khandker (1998). The impact of group-based credit programs on poor households in Bangladesh: Does the gender of participants matter? *Journal of Political Economy*, 106, 958–996.

Pitt, M.M., S.R. Khandker, & J. Cartwright (2006). Empowering women with micro finance: Evidence from Bangladesh. *Economic Development and Cultural Change*, 54(4), 791–831.

Pratto, F., & Walker, A. (2004). The Bases of Gendered Power, in A.H. Eagly, A.E. Beall, & R.J. Sternberg (eds), *The Psychology of Gender*, The Guilford Press, New York, 242–268.

Queen Máxima of the Netherlands (2021). Supporting SMEs and women-owned businesses to bounce back better. Speech, Side-Event Proposal for the Italian G20 Leaders' Summit, Rome.

Rahman, A. (1999). Micro-credit initiatives for equitable and sustainable development: Who pays?, *World Development*, 27(1), 67–82. https://doi.org/10.1016/s0305-750x(98)00105-3

Ray, D. (2006). Aspirations, Poverty and Economic Change. In Abhijit V. Banerjee, Roland Benabou and Dilip Mookherjee (Eds.), *Understanding Poverty* (pp. 409–422). Oxford: Oxford University Press.

Riley, E. (2017). Role models in movies: The impact of Queen of Katwe on students' educational attainment, CSAE Working Paper Series 2017-13, Oxford University. https://ideas.repec.org/p/csa/wpaper/2017-13.html

Robinson, J. (1952). *The Generalization of the General Theory: The Rate of Interest and Other Essays*, Macmillan, London.

Robinson, M.S. (2001). *The Microfinance Revolution: Sustainable Finance for the Poor*, World Bank, Washington, DC.

Roodman, D., & J. Morduch (2014). The impact of microcredit on the poor in Bangladesh: Revisiting the evidence. *Journal of Development Studies*, 50(4), 583–605.

Rosenberg, M. (1965). *Society and the Adolescent Self-image*, Princeton University Press, Princeton, NJ.

Rousseau, P. L., & P. Wachtel (2011). What is happening to the impact of financial deepening on economic growth? *Economic Inquiry*, 49(1), 276–288.

Rühmann, F., S. Konda, P. Horrocks, & N. Taka (2020). Can blockchain technology reduce the cost of remittances? *OECD Development Co-operation Working Papers*, No. 73, OECD Publishing, Paris, https://doi.org/10.1787/d4d6ac8f-en.

Said, F., M. Mahmud, G. d'Adda, & A. Chaudhry (2021). Home-based enterprises: Experimental evidence on female preferences from Pakistan. *Economic Development and Cultural Change*. https://doi.org/10.1086/714739.

Sarma, M. (2008). Index of Financial Inclusion. *ICRIER Working Paper*, August.

Sarma, M., & J. Pais (2011). Financial inclusion and development. *Journal of International Development*, 23, 613–628.

Schaner, S. (2017). The cost of convenience? Transaction costs, bargaining power, and savings account use in Kenya. *Journal of Human Resources*, 52(4), 919–945.

Sen, A. (1992). Missing women. *British Medical Journal*, 304(6827), 587–588. doi: 10.1136/bmj.304.6827.587

Sengupta, R., & C. Aubuchon (2008). The microfinance revolution: An overview. *Review*, 90, 9–30. 10.20955/r.90.9-30.

Siba, E. (2019). Empowering women entrepreneurs in developing countries: Why current programs fall short, Africa Growth Institute Policy Brief, Brookings India. http://hdl.handle.net/11540/9976.

Somville, V. & L. Vandewalle (2018). Saving by default: Evidence from a field experiment in rural India. *American Economic Journal: Applied Economics*, 10(3); 39–66.

Stiglitz, J.E., & A. Weiss (1981). Credit rationing in markets with imperfect information. *American Economic Review*, 71(3), 393–410.

Suesse, M., & N. Wolf (2020). Rural transformation, inequality, and the origins of microfinance. *Journal of Development Economics*, 143, 102429.

Sulaiman, M., N. Goldberg, D. Karlan, & A. de Montesquiou (2016). Eliminating Extreme Poverty: Comparing the Cost-Effectiveness of Livelihood, Cash Transfer, and Graduation Approaches. CGAP Report No. 11.

Suri, T., & W. Jack (2016). The long-run poverty and gender impacts of mobile money. *Science*, 354(6317): 1288–1292.

Swamy, V. (2014). Financial inclusion, gender dimension, and economic impact on poor households. *World Development*, 56(C), 1–15.

Tarozzi, A., J. Desai, & K. Johnson (2015). The impacts of microcredit: Evidence from Ethiopia. *American Economic Journal: Applied Economics*, 7(1), 54–89.

Todd, B. (2017). Is it fair to say that most social programmes don't work? [Blog] Retrieved from https://80000hours.org/articles/effective-social-program/

Tyson, J., & T. Beck (2018). *Capital Flows and Financial Sector Development in Low-Income Countries*. degrp.odi.org. Growth Research Programme. Synthesis Report.

Udry, C. (1996). Gender, agricultural production, and the theory of the household. *Journal of Political Economy*, 104(5), 1010–1046.

UN Women (2021). *Impact of COVID-19 on Gender Equality and Women's Empowerment in East and Southern Africa*. UN.

USAID (2018). *Report: Microenterprise and Pathways out of Poverty*. US Agency for International Development.

Vaessen, J., A. Rivas, M. Duvendack, R. Jones, F. Leeuw, & G. Gils, et al. (2014). The effects of microcredit on women's control over household spending in developing countries: A systematic review and meta-analysis. *Campbell Systematic Reviews*, 10(1), 1–205. https://doi.org/10.4073/csr.2014.8

van Dongen, E., Ahmad, S., Lensink, R., and A. Mueller (2022). Trapped by the lack of control over savings: Evidence from Pakistan. *Frontiers in Psychology*. https://doi.org/10.3389/fpsyg.2022.867841 (in press)

van Rooyen, C., R. Stewart, & T. de Wet (2012). The impact of microfinance in Sub-Saharan Africa: A systematic review of the evidence. *World Development*, 40, 2249–2262.

Williamson, J. (1990). *Latin American Adjustment: How Much Has Happened?* Institute for International Economics, Washington, DC.

Williamson, J. (2004). The strange history of the Washington Consensus. *Journal of Post Keynesian Economics*, 27(2), 195–206. Retrieved April 29, 2021, from http://www.jstor.org/stable/4538920

World Bank (2011). World Development Report 2012: Gender Equality and Development. World Bank Report.

World Bank (2018). *UFA2020 Overview: Universal Financial Access by 2020.* Retrieved from https://www.worldbank.org/en/topic/financialinclusion/brief/achieving-universal-financial-access-by-2020

World Bank (2019). *Women, Business, and the Law: A Decade of Reform.* World Bank Report.

Xu, Xiaoyan (2020). Trust and financial inclusion: A cross-country study. *Finance Research Letters*, 35, 101310.

Yermack, D. (2018). Fintech in Sub-Saharan Africa: What has worked well, and what hasn't. National Bureau of Economic Research (NBER) Working Paper 25007. http://www.nber.org/papers/w25007

Young, A. (1995). The tyranny of numbers: Confronting the statistical realities of the East Asian growth experience. *Quarterly Journal of Economics*, 110(3), 641–680.

Zagorsky, J. (2021). Bitcoin is now 'legal tender' in El Salvador – here's what that means. *The Conversation.* Retrieved from https://theconversation.com/bitcoin-is-now-legal-tender-in-el-salvador-heres-what-that-means-167099

Zavolokina, L., M. Dolata, & G. Schwabe (2016). FinTech—What's in a name? In *Proceedings of the Thirty Seventh International Conference on Information Systems*, Dublin, Ireland, 469–490.

Zeldes, S. P. (1989). Consumption and liquidity constraints: An empirical investigation. *Journal of Political Economy*, 97(2), 305–346.

Zheng, Z., S. Xie, H. Dai, X. Chen, & H. Wang (2018). Blockchain challenges and opportunities: A survey. *International Journal of Web and Grid Services*, 14(4), 352–375.

Zins, A., & L. Weill (2016). The determinants of financial inclusion in Africa. *Review of Development Finance*, 6, 46–57.

Index

Titles in the **Elgar Advanced Introductions** series include: